How to Deal with the
Cares
of Life

Charles Cowan

Unless otherwise indicated, all Scripture quotations in this volume are from the *King James Version* of the Bible.

First Printing 2004

ISBN 0-89276-969-6

In the U.S. write:
Kenneth Hagin Ministries
P.O. Box 50126
Tulsa, OK 74150-0126
1-888-28-FAITH
www.rhema.org

In Canada write:
Kenneth Hagin Ministries
P.O. Box 335, Station D
Etobicoke (Toronto), Ontario
Canada, M9A 4X3

Contents

Introduction

We are living in the greatest moment the Body of Christ will know in the earth, for this is the day of the end-time harvest when millions of souls will be swept into the Kingdom of God. Signs, wonders, and miracles of God's power and might will be confirming the Holy Scripture of God. And if you are in your place, He is going to use you in a way that you never dreamed possible. The Bible says you will have His power flowing from your innermost being. And God is going to fill your mouth and cause you to talk to people with wisdom they can't withstand. The gainsayer shall have to conclude that you are anointed by the Spirit of God!

We are the generation that will see the coming of the Lord, face to face. Whoever will blow the horn is licking his lips today. He has the horn to his mouth and he is getting ready to blow . . . and we are getting ready to see the Lord of lords and the King of kings! We are getting ready to see the Messiah of all the people—the Redeemer of all humanity of all the ages! Soon He will descend from Heaven in all of His glory and power, coming down on a cloud to receive us up to Himself.

However, that being so, we can be sure that Satan is not idle. The Bible warns us that as we come to the time of God's last great push for souls, Satan will not be lying back, conceding the thwarting of his plots. He remembers his crushing defeat at Jesus' hand, and he knows he is headed for the bottomless pit, the lake of fire—but he has not surrendered to that. Today, he is trying to overcharge you with the cares of this life so that God's power can't flow through you. He wants to keep you stressed out.

My purpose in writing this book is to set forth spiritual principles that will help you resist the cares of life. By following these biblical truths, you will be strengthened and empowered to triumph—you can live above the pressures of life!

It is obvious in the Scriptures that Jesus does not want any of His people burdened and loaded with care. He went to great lengths to provide everything that you and I, and every other born-again Christian need to overcome anything that might take us out of our place in God. If you will take hold of and practice the biblical message of this book, it will help keep you in a state of readiness for the soon coming of our Lord and Savior Jesus Christ.

An urgent hour has come for Christians to be leaders of hope and power. It is time for each of us to be in position for these final days. From the following pages, you can glean priceless insight that will enable you to know your rightful place in God's Kingdom and how to stay there.

Let's start right now finding out how to do that. As you finish each chapter, take it to heart; apply it to your life. We can't afford to allow the cares of life to keep us burdened down. We must lift up our heads, for our redemption is drawing nigh. We must be ready!

1

Laden With Cares

As I look out across the world today, the magnitude of stress is one of the most disturbing things I see. People are stressed out with all kinds of circumstances. They are dealing with circumstances about their children, their jobs and businesses, and their relationships. Many are dealing with just the nitty-gritty of living, and they are stressed out about it.

Unfortunately, this stress is not only prevalent in the world, but it is just as prevalent in the Body of Christ. Sunday after Sunday, Christians come into churches across America—and across the world—and sit in the pews, their lives laden with care. Sometimes the cares of life have burdened them to such a degree that they can't give attention to the Word of God, even at church. Their mind is too encumbered with all they are dealing with in life.

The cares of life come at us from all sides, and if they are allowed to, they can cause full-blown stress, which can grow to be overwhelming and can devastate us emotionally, mentally, physically—and financially.

But what does God have to say about that? Should Christians be stressed? Shouldn't they, of all people, know how to deal with the cares of life?

What Is Stress?

You might not need me to define the word *stress* for you. In fact, you might already be thinking, *If I don't know what* stress *means, I surely know what it feels like.* Nevertheless, pinpointing what stress is can help us understand how to overcome it.

Stress is the body's specific response to an external stimulus that affects your thoughts and feelings. Any negative external stimulus can be called the cares of life. So, simply put, being overstressed is the by-product of yielding to, or giving in to, the cares of life.

Fear's Part

Most often, *fear* introduces us to the cares of life. Somewhere in the midst of their circumstances, people develop a fear of something. It might be something as simple as a fear of not being in control of their home—

and the direction it's going—or, perhaps, a fear of not having enough resources to meet the responsibilities of life.

Whatever its means of introduction, fear comes to the children of God and begins to weave its way into the very fabric of their thoughts and feelings until they take on the *care* of that which they fear. And sometimes, that care weighs on them and sits on them and brings them into a place of stress where they can barely function from day to day. They get out of bed dreading to go to work, dreading to face life, wishing they could just stay *in* bed and cover their head. When stress reaches this point, we call it depression.

Stress that reaches this extent is designed to rob you. It will steal from you and can *kill* you. Getting its hold mainly through fear, it becomes an instrument in Satan's hand to keep you from having the joy of the Lord in your life. Satan knows the joy of the Lord strengthens you and will help you defeat him.

A Joyful Heart

Life presents many obstacles that sometimes may seem insurmountable, but God wants you to have joy despite that. The obstacles in your life might seem to be walls you can never get over. Even so, God wants you to have joy when the walls are up and joy when the walls are down. It might seem that you are constantly in and out of the storms of life. Still, God wants you to have joy when the wind is blowing, when it's raining, or when it's thundering—and God wants you to have joy when the sun is shining. But fear can stand in the way of that, if you allow it.

Fear does not come from God. Second Timothy 1:7 says, *"For God hath not given us the spirit of fear; but of power, and of love, and of a sound mind."* This verse shows us that any fear that opposes God's gift to us of power, love, and a sound mind is a *spirit*. That kind of fear bears all the earmarks of the devil—it comes to steal, kill, and destroy.

Not all forms of fear are destructive, however. For example, the Bible mentions the fear of God, but that kind of fear is a reverence or a reverential fear whereby we respect and honor Him.

Fear also has another healthy side: caution. For instance, if you are at an intersection and ready to cross the street, you need to go across with caution. So before you walk into the street, you look both ways to decide if anything is moving dangerously toward you.

Reverential fear and caution are wise elements of fear, and it is easy to see that they are healthy types of fear that differ from a *spirit* of fear. Satan introduces the spirit of fear to lead people into taking upon themselves the cares of life—and the stress those cares bring. He intends to use fear to rob people of God's blessings. But God wants the joy of the Lord to be so big in you that it keeps all destructive fear away from your life. He wants you to have a sound mind, not a troubled mind that fears the next bad thing that *might* happen.

Frightened Out of One's Senses

Fear is a powerful emotion that can show up overwhelmingly—and unannounced. It can make itself right at home in your life, sometimes producing sudden opportunities for you to take on high levels of stress.

One level of fear carries the meaning "frightened out of one's senses." Have you ever experienced that? Have you ever been so frightened that you couldn't think straight? I have.

One cold December day, I was on an airplane going from Nashville to Dallas. The plane took off and leveled at a certain altitude, but as we moved along, it suddenly plunged downward. I didn't know *what* was happening, but it felt as if the plane went into a nosedive—that plane was going down!

The next thing I knew, this *fear* came up into my throat. And it didn't get any better when the captain, with a strong note of urgency in his voice, came on the intercom, saying, "Flight attendants, return to your seats immediately and buckle your seat belts!"

The sudden descent lasted only a few seconds, I'm sure, but it felt as though it went on forever! Fear filled the plane with a gripping silence.

After we had descended for a bit, the plane began to level off, but by then it was also shaking from strong turbulence. The pilot spoke on the intercom again, this time to explain, "Ladies and gentlemen, we have experienced some problems in the cockpit. The windshield has cracked!" It turned out that the pilot had quickly taken the plane down to a lower altitude so we could still breathe if the cabin depressurized!

The problem was, when he brought the plane down to a lower altitude, we flew right into an eastward-moving storm of freezing rain. Trying to ease our mind, the pilot again spoke on the intercom: "We are eighty miles from Little Rock, Arkansas. We will land there." He assured us that everything was all right, but about two minutes later, he came back on, saying, "Ladies and gentlemen, we have just been informed that the Little Rock airport is *closed* because of the storm."

I'm telling you, fear was sitting in my lap! And the pilot didn't help the situation any when he gave us the next update. I'm sure he didn't mean it the way it sounded to me, but through the muffled crackle of the intercom, he said, "We're going to try to make it to the Dallas/Fort Worth airport."

The first thought that entered my lightning-fast mind was, *You don't "try" to make it up here; you either do it or you don't.* At an altitude of 10,000 feet, we flew in a relentless ice storm all the way to Dallas . . . with a cracked windshield!

Obviously, we made it.

Have 'God Sense'

At times like that, if you don't know how to handle extreme and sudden fear, you will allow it to frighten you out of your senses. By that, I mean it will frighten you to such a degree that you will not think as you should in a crisis—which is just the reaction Satan wants to cause in you when he introduces the spirit of fear into your life. He is trying to frighten you out of your senses to knock you off your faith in God.

When I talk about your senses, I'm talking about your "God senses"—the mind of Christ in you, or the renewed spirit of your mind. Satan tries to frighten you out of your senses so that you don't think as you should, because any fearful thoughts you have—if you express them in words—will lend themselves to what he has come to do. But your "God senses" oppose that, helping you to think in line with what God said He has *already* done.

Let me give you an example. When that plane took a nosedive, Satan said to me, "This plane is going down! You are going to die!" But before anything ever happened on that flight, I knew that God had already said He had given His angels charge over me.

PSALM 91:11,12

11 **For he shall give his angels charge over thee, to keep thee in all thy ways.**

12 **They shall bear thee up in their hands, lest thou dash thy foot against a stone.**

I also knew that God had already said any weapon formed against me would not work. And I knew I didn't have to listen to what Satan had to say because Isaiah 54:17 says, *"No weapon that is formed against thee shall prosper; and every tongue that shall rise against thee in judgment thou shalt condemn."*

Satan comes to frighten Christians out of their senses so they don't think in line with the Word of God. If he can get us to take enough fear, our words will become contrary to what God's Word says and, consequently, our actions will become contrary to the way God would have us act.

Thank God for the spirit of power, love, and a sound mind! We have that—in Christ. But it's up to us to yield to that truth when fear shows up. (And we already know, fear *will* show up.)

What's on Your Mind?

Before His ascension, Jesus said, *"Peace I leave with you, my peace I give unto you . . . . Let not your heart be troubled, neither let it be afraid"* (John 14:27). In this verse, Jesus passed the responsibility to us to walk in His provision of peace and *see to it* that our hearts are not troubled.

As we battle against the cares of life, it's crucial for us to know that a troubled heart begins with troubled thoughts. Our mind is like a tape recorder and our thoughts are like a long tape recording. Whatever is on our tape will play in every situation we face.)

Satan will bring negative circumstances with our family, our friends, or any other area of our personal life where he is able to work. These circumstances may not be of our making. Nonetheless, we must deal with them. We might not want to deal with them, but we just have to do it.

Sometimes, however, the stress and care is of our own making. Either way, the cares immediately press the play button of the tape recorder in our mind and our mind begins to play whatever is on the tape.

If the Word of God is on the tape but we fail to deal with the care according to the Word, then that care will erase the tape and steal the Word of God away from us. We will be nothing more than _religious_—knowing what the Word of God says, yet disconnected from any spiritual power. We can go to church every Sunday or every time the doors open, for that matter, but still be void of any spiritual power.

Faith's Arena

Have you ever felt as though things are so bad that you just want to sit down and have a good cry? Well, your faith, not your crying, defeats the cares of life. Your pity parties will not defeat them.

Now I understand that life can become tough and problems can be severe, and I understand that people can easily get into a situation where it looks as if crying is the best thing to do. I'm not saying you shouldn't cry; I'm saying that crying is not the way out. You may feel better when you sit down and cry. It may be an emotional release for you, but unless you inject the faith of God into your crying, crying alone will not get you out of the cares of life.

If you focus on the cares of life, they will weigh you down and make you want to cry. They will sit right up on your shoulder and burden you down. They will make you believe that God has forsaken you and is not hearing you. They will make you believe that He doesn't love you. You will go through a whole broad range of emotions and thoughts until you learn how to deal with your mind as soon as the cares of life show up.

Your mind is the arena of combat between the cares of life and the faith of God. One or the other will win, depending on the decisions *you* make. No preacher, pastor, minister, prophet, or apostle can make those decisions for you. Absolutely no one can make those decisions but you. And you can't get into a prayer line and have someone lay hands on you and pray a renewed mind into you so you can make the right decisions.

Romans 10:17 says, *"So then faith cometh by hearing, and hearing by the word of God."* To live a life of faith, you have to get your mind between the covers of the Bible until your mind is so washed with the Word of God that every time someone or some situation squeezes you, the Word pops out. You need to be like a sponge so full of water that when it is lightly touched or squeezed, the water squirts out. Get yourself so full of the Word and your mind so renewed to the Word that when Satan comes and punches you with a care, the Word squirts out of your heart and mouth.

It is solely your responsibility to put the Word first place in your life so that it becomes first place in your thinking. The Apostle Paul taught us about that.

Writing to the Colossians, he said, *"Set your affection on things above, not on things on the earth. For ye are dead, and your life is hid with Christ in God"* (Col. 3:2,3). When he said to set your affection, he meant to set your *mind* on things above. Set your mind on God, not on your cares.

Are You Carnal or Spiritual?

Whatever goes on in your mind controls the level of peace you enjoy. Romans 8:6 and 7 says, *". . . To be carnally minded is death; but to be spiritually minded is life and peace. Because the carnal mind is enmity against God: for it is not subject to the law of God, neither indeed can be."*

As you can see, your mind can go to two extremes— to life and peace or to death. Paul says being *carnally* minded, or naturally minded, is death. To be naturally minded is to think the way some people think based only on what they see in the natural realm. In other words, they think in line with what they see in the cir- cumstances around them, without involving God and His Word in their thoughts.

Paul goes on to say, *". . . but to be spiritually minded is life and peace."* So what does it mean to be *spiritually* minded? It means to have the mind of the Spirit and not act in the natural, which is the vantage point of the carnal mind. It means, as verse 7 explains, that we yield our thoughts to the spiritual laws of God, allowing

Him and His Word to work and bring life and peace
into our circumstances.

Vaccinate Your Mind

You can't be spiritually minded unless you have the
mind of the Spirit. Jesus tells us in John's account of
the Gospel, *". . . The words that I speak unto you, they
are spirit, and they are life"* (John 6:63).

From this verse, we see that to have the mind of
the Spirit, we must have the mind of the Word of God.
The Word of God is the mind of God, so the Word of
God is the mind of the Spirit. We have to bring our
thoughts and our mind under subjection to the Word of
God to the extent that we renew the spirit of our mind.
We must leave that carnal mind, or way of thinking,
and allow the Word of God to be the thinking of our
mind. In so doing, we become spiritually minded, and
life and peace can be around and about us to lift us up
in every situation.

If we are diligent to renew our mind to the Word,
then when Satan huffs and puffs and blows upon our
life, or when potential danger and devastation are near,
we can take God's thoughts into our mind. We can say,
"No! Trouble will not come near me!" How are we able
to say that? Because when we take God's thoughts, it
means that we have vaccinated our mind with His
Word. And that means when trouble comes, it encoun-

ters God's vaccine, which has built great resistance in us. Trouble has no choice but to go elsewhere.

If we are going to deal successfully with the cares of life, we must teach ourselves to think according to God's Word. For instance, when that plane took a nose-dive, fear came rushing into my mind with its thoughts of death and destruction, but I made a decision not to allow my mind to think carnal thoughts. The Word of God quickly displaced the thoughts of fear, because I practice renewing my mind daily with the Word of God. Because of that, I have the mind of the Spirit to see me through in the face of fear. (Anyone can have that by meditating on the Word of God.)

One of the main weapons Satan uses to frighten us out of our senses is to bring so much fear about some-thing that we take the care of it upon ourselves. When we do that, we move God over to the side where He no longer has a voice and position in the circumstance. If we allow that to happen, we are trying alone to fix whatever it is that is coming against our life. We are left alone to work our way through it or bear up under it. In essence, we have made a choice not to have the mind of the Spirit, choosing instead to give in to our carnal thinking, which is unto death, according to Paul's writings. (_See_ Rom. 8:6.)

As that plane plunged thousands of feet toward the ground, death was already knocking at my door; I didn't need to invite it in.

Stay Balanced

We can see that care is a distraction of the mind to cause one's thinking to be out of balance. This imbalance is known as stress. If we don't deal with care from its onset, we become stressed out. People say, "I'm stressed and I can't do anything about it." Yes, you *can* do something about it. Stress is introduced to you by the cares of this world left unchallenged between your ears.

If you choose not to deal with the care in your mind, Satan is going to come into your house and take the guest bedroom, and his next move will be into *your* bedroom! If you leave that rascal in the house, he will come with you to the kitchen and the bathroom, he will get in the car with you, and he will go into the backyard with you while you are grilling. You might be cooking and, all of a sudden, your mind will be a thousand miles away, meditating on the cares of this world.

If you don't deal with cares, they will deal with you. Don't get the idea that trying to ignore them will help. The cares of life don't go away just because we ignore them. You might become hardened to them if you ignore them, but they won't just go away. You must deal with the cares of life as soon as they come to your mind to wage war in your thinking. You must know and believe the Word and use it as a weapon against the cares of life.

Second Corinthians 10:3–5 says, *"For though we walk in the flesh, we do not war after the flesh: (For the weapons of our warfare are not carnal, but mighty through God to the pulling down of strong holds;) Casting down imaginations, and every high thing that exalteth itself against the knowledge of God, and bringing into captivity every thought to the obedience of Christ."*

The word *carnal* in the preceding passage refers not only to the flesh but also to whatever is in the soul of a person who is weak and tends toward the ungodly. The word *ungodly* sometimes makes us think of the worst sin scenario we can conjure up. But when I use the word *ungodly*, I'm talking about *anything* that is unlike God. Whatever is ungodly, or unlike God, is carnal.

Carnality in the life of a Christian will produce the influence of spiritual death. And none of us is exempt from the effects of carnality if we allow the cares of life to determine how we think. This includes those of us who go to church every week and hear the Word on a continuing basis. We can sit in church while the Word is preached, yet allow our mind to be so consumed with the cares of life that we can't even pay attention.

The cares of life can take away that which is most important in our life. In the parable of the sower, Jesus taught about the power of the cares of life.

MARK 4:18,19

18 And these are they which are sown among thorns; such as hear the word,

19 And the cares of this world, and the deceitfulness of riches, and the lusts of other things entering in, choke the word, and it becometh unfruitful.

In verse 18, the verb tense of "hear" in the original Greek means that it is an ongoing action. So Jesus is not talking to people who have heard the Word one or two times; He is talking to people who have had opportunity to hear the Word continually.

Notice that something else is going on here during this process of continually hearing the Word. Jesus says in verse 19, *"AND the cares of this world . . . ."* Here He points out that while people are hearing the Word, they also are thinking about their cares. In other words, it is not as if they come and receive the Word, walk out the door, and *then* the cares of life come. No, *while* they are hearing the Word, these people are dealing with the cares of life. The Word and the cares of life are competing for the listeners' attention.

Many times, while people are sitting in a service where the Word is being preached, care distracts them so much that they leave the service—not physically, but mentally—and then they come back to listen again. And they don't hear anything in that gap of time.

Jesus, the All-Knowing Lord, says here that the cares of life will choke the Word and cause it to be unfruitful. He has given us a warning that we should take to heart, and we should deal with the cares of life accordingly.

Between Your Ears

Everything that brings care into your life is designed to draw your attention away from the Word of God. For instance, the devil may try to stir up a person to do hurtful things to you. That attack is designed to capture your attention. And it is designed in a negative way so that it will stay between your ears—you can hardly stop thinking about it. And, although you say you have forgiven that person, if you have an opportunity to tell someone else what you have forgiven him or her of, you will tell it.

You may say, "I forgave them many months ago, but did I tell you what they did?" Or you may say, "I want you to know that I love them and I'm praying for them, but I have to tell you how badly they treated me." When you find yourself overcharged with the cares of life like this, your mind is occupied. A war is going on between your ears, even though you know what the Word of God says about forgiveness.

It's War!

In wartime, stronger nations invade smaller, weaker nations and occupy their land. Those strong nations have occupation forces or troops there to bring that land and territory under their rule. However, the land doesn't belong to them.

That situation is similar to what goes on in your mind when Satan captures your attention. Satan moves in on your mind to set up shop and occupy it with the cares of this life and to function and operate in a territory that is not his. It doesn't belong to him. Enforce your authority—and run him off!

The Apostle Paul tells you in Second Corinthians 10:5 how to put the devil on the run. He writes, *"Casting down imaginations, and every high thing that exalteth itself against the knowledge of God, and bringing into captivity every thought to the obedience of Christ."*

When negative thoughts are not brought into captivity, they will become a care. They will occupy the territory of your mind. They are invading forces that are sent to occupy territory that does not belong to them. They will set up camp and pitch their tent in your mind.

Captivity

These negative thoughts, once they occupy your mind in the form of the cares of this life, can become strongholds in your life. And strongholds can lead to physical captivity. Once negative thoughts become embedded in a person's mind, the cares of this life introduce stress, worry, and anxiety, and if left unattended in the mind, they will cause sickness and disease.

For instance, stress and anxiety sometimes can cause blood pressure to go sky high. Sniffles can become more prevalent. People may say, "I never had colds before. I never got sick. But now, and I don't understand why, suddenly I'm getting sick a lot." Well, it is easy to understand why. The cares of this life produce negative thinking, and that produces stress in your life, and being overstressed causes physical ailments.

Sickness, disease, depression—all of these can come when Satan oppresses your mind with negative thinking. If you leave negative thoughts there and dwell on them, they will get into your mind and develop to the point where, suddenly, the devil is controlling what, and how you think. When you allow him to do that, he is also controlling the way you talk and how you act. All of this evolves from the cares of this life.

You are a spirit (that is the part of your being that has been born again), but you still have a soul and you still live in a body—and you will have all three until you leave your body. To deal with the cares of life, you must do something with your soul, which includes your mind, will, and emotions. Whatever you do with your soul (specifically, your mind), you will find that your body will tag along with it.

Pulling Down Strongholds

Satan seeks to use your mind to set up strongholds in your life. If he can get you thinking about something negative and *keep* you thinking about it long enough, some weakness in your soul will grab hold of it. It will begin to manifest itself as a care, troubling your mind and keeping your thoughts occupied with everything but God. When you think about carnal things more than about God, those carnal things are strongholds.

Sometimes we notice something about ourselves, such as a bad habit, but we don't realize it is a stronghold. The symptoms of a stronghold can be, for instance, smoking or overeating, but those actions come from a stronghold in the mind. The symptoms are not the root of the problem; the stronghold is.

In other words, if Satan wants you to become addicted to drugs, he doesn't start off by getting you to smoke a cigarette or a joint. No, first he builds a stronghold *in your mind*. You always have a thought about something *before* you do it.

Some people say, "Brother Charles, I just can't quit overeating." Where is that thought coming from? It is coming out of their mind. What has happened? That troubled state of mind, or care, however it has been introduced by the enemy, has gotten a stronghold in their life. It has taken root. They are now convinced that even God can't help them. They say, "Well, God _could_ help me if He would, but I'm not sure whether He will."

That kind of thinking is doubt. These people will do externally what has already become a stronghold in their mind. For instance, someone who has been trying to stop overeating may go to the table and eat three plates full, then push back from the table and say, "I wasn't going to do that again. Next week I'm going to the weight loss place." In this case, food itself is not their problem; the stronghold in their mind is the problem.

Smoking addiction is another example: Though the body becomes addicted to nicotine, the problem is first in the mind. Your body will do what your mind makes it do.

Second Corinthians 10:4 says that our weapons are _". . . mighty through God to the pulling down of strong holds."_ What does that mean? A stronghold will eventually lead to something negative in your life, so pulling down a stronghold means you must bring negative thoughts under subjection to the Word.

At times, strongholds develop in those who hear the Word continually because, while they are listening to it, they are looking the preacher right in the eye and rehearsing the care in their mind.

You must make a quality decision that while you are at church, your mind is reserved for that certain number of minutes only for the Word and thoughts of God. Every time a care tries to enter your mind, you smack it right out the door and leave it outside on the doorstep. But know that it will be there waiting for you. It won't get into your car, and it won't walk to your house. It will be right there at the door when you leave church. Refuse to pick it up on your way out!

Spiritual Thinking

P eople have a misconception about the cares of
life. Some even teach that the cares of life are
designed to make us more responsible. When
the cares of life show up, these people say, "You know, I
would be concerned if I *didn't* have a care about it. Why,
if I *didn't* worry about it, I would be irresponsible."
Others think that bearing up year after year under the
same problems is a sign of humility.

Don't make the mistake of thinking that care will
develop responsibility or humility in you. (We will look
more at what Bible humility is in a later chapter.)
Instead, the cares of life will steal the Word out of your
life. Satan wants to steal the Word because he knows
the Word will produce peace for you.

Only a spiritual mind can deal successfully with the
cares of life. Check yourself. If you are not thinking

spiritually, then you are going to be laden with the cares of life, stressed out, and full of anxiety.

Only the Word of God gives you the mind of the Spirit or, in other words, makes you spiritually minded. Contrary to what some teach, outward things don't do it. It is not the length or style of your hair or the way you dress that makes you spiritually minded. (Although sometimes I wonder if some people have *any* mind, considering what they wear.) What we have *in* our mind makes us either spiritual or carnal. Our *thinking* leads us either to life or to death. Being spiritually minded means that we have the Word of God first place in our mind when trouble comes.

Don't Choke

At the moment trouble comes, if you let the Word slip away, you will have nothing in your life that will produce for you what God says belongs to you. If the cares of this world *enter in* to your thinking, they will choke the power of the Word. It is your choice what you allow to enter in.

People often deal with stress by pulling back from God. They begin to think, *I need to lessen my responsibilities where God is concerned; I need to step back and get a deep breath.* Then they remove themselves from prayer, the Word, speaking the Word, tithing, and going to church because they are so distracted with care. They pull back because of the stress.

That is the wrong approach to use to defeat your problems. If you are stressed and pulling back from God, you are making matters worse. You should put on your running shoes and run _toward_ the Word as fast as you can, because Satan is setting you up so he can strike a deathblow in your life. If he doesn't kill you physically, he will rob you of the joy of living. He will rob you of your peace; He will rob you of your needs being met. He will rob you of _all_ the blessings that God wants to give you. Satan will take all of that away from you if you pull away from God and His Word.

Receive Power

We should thank God for His Word. We should give Him praise and glory for the power of the Word. The Word of God is a lamp unto our feet and light unto our path (Ps. 119:105). The prophet of old said he found God's words and did eat them, and they were unto him the joy and rejoicing of his heart (Jer. 15:16). The psalmist David knew the priceless value of God's words.

PSALM 19:8–10

8   **The statutes of the Lord are right, rejoicing the heart: the commandment of the Lord is pure, enlightening the eyes.**

9   **The fear of the Lord is clean, enduring forever: the judgments of the Lord are true and righteous altogether.**

10   **More to be desired are they than gold, yea, than much fine gold: sweeter also than honey and the honeycomb.**

The Lord Jesus also told us of the importance of God's words. Luke 4:4 says, *"And Jesus answered him, saying, It is written, That man shall not live by bread alone, but by every word of God."*

These verses tell us how to have a life filled with the power of God so that God's power moves us out of and away from those things that Satan has designed to destroy our life. We must feed ourselves the Word of God.

God's Word is precious and wonderful, and Jeremiah, the Old Testament prophet, tells us that God promised to perform it: *"Then said the Lord unto me, Thou hast well seen: for I will hasten my word to perform it"* (Jer. 1:12). The word *hasten* means "to watch over."

Unlike some people you may know, God is serious about keeping His word. When He tells you in His Word that you were healed by the stripes laid on Jesus' back, He wants you to realize that He will stand behind His word and see to it that you are healed. All He asks is that you believe His Word and trust Him to do it. He watches over every word of His that you believe so that He can bring it to pass for you.

Your Bible is the Word of God. Every word in it is God speaking to you. It is unfailing, infallible, and the truth above all books. Unleashing the power of the Word into your life will set you free from the cares of life.

Don't Trip the Breaker

One of the first steps in dealing with the cares of life is to realize that you can't handle everything in life by yourself. Right now, you might be thinking, *I know. I tried everything I knew to do, and then I had to get someone to pray.*

You can't handle everything by yourself, and your brothers and sisters in the Body of Christ can't handle them for you either. They can't live between your ears. What goes on between your ears is strictly what *you* let go on there.

God can handle everything in your life—with your cooperation. But when you try to handle the cares of life alone, they create an overload; they stress you out. The more you struggle with them, the more you become stressed out. You won't feel like getting out of bed in the morning. You will blow your fuse.

I don't mean that in the sense of people getting angry and "blowing their fuse." The cares of life will blow your fuse, just as an electrical overload will blow a fuse in the fuse box or trip the breaker in the electrical panel in your house.

When an electrical circuit is overloaded, a fuse blows or a breaker trips. At that moment, the circuit disconnects from the power supply. And if a breaker trips in your electrical system at home, nothing on that circuit will work until the problem is fixed and the power is connected again.

Many Christians are going around today disconnected from God's power, yet they are still talking about how they believe God. They say, "Yes, sir, I believe the Word." Nevertheless, they are going here and yonder disconnected from His power, having no flow in their life, laden with a load of care, struggling from day to day and never able to get a breakthrough.

Are you ready for a breakthrough? Then let's go on to see more of how to do that.

Bigger Than Our Cares

C are is a thief of the Word, but care will steal the Word only if you allow it in. You must stay alert, watch for care, and not allow it in. The cares of life come in many different packages, including, for instance, the package of financial pressures. Too often, people take upon themselves the care of their job (or business) and its financial uncertainty. But it is important that we understand something—*our job is not our source*. It is a channel or an instrument God uses, but if we look at it as our only source to meet our financial needs, then our job becomes our god. If our business is our source, then our business becomes our god.

God is bigger than any business, any job, and any financial care, as long as you know that God—and God alone—is your source of provision. You must come to the place where you say, "Let no man say he has made me rich, but God, and God alone. For I am a covenant man and my God meets my need according to His riches in glory by Christ Jesus" (*see* Gen. 14:22,23; Phil. 4:19).

God is not only bigger than any problem you might have on your job or in your business, He is also bigger than problems with your children, your spouse, or any sickness or disease. He is bigger than the worry. He is bigger than the anxiety. God is bigger than anything you are dealing with today. *He is bigger!*

God meets our needs. He is our Helper, and we should not fear what man shall do to us. God is BIG! He is Mighty God. He is El Shaddai. He is Jehovah Jireh!

Bible Humility

Bible humility is another matter of importance that we must understand in order to successfully overcome the cares of life. But, contrary to what some people think, Bible humility is not just bearing the same cares year after year without complaining. Let's look at the following to see what the Bible says about true humility.

First Peter 5:6 and 7 says, *"Humble yourselves therefore under the mighty hand of God, that he may exalt you in due time: Casting all your care upon him; for he careth for you."*

Peter says in this passage of Scripture that we must "humble" ourselves. That means it is needless to ask others to pray that God will humble us, and it is

needless for us to pray that God will humble us. No, the
Word says, "Humble *yourselves!*" Now why does God
want us to be humble? He has a desire for our life: He
wants to exalt us.

When being exalted is mentioned, many people
think, *Here we go with that religious stuff again.* They
don't like to hear about being exalted. They shy away
from exalting or being exalted because they have been
taught that God doesn't want us to be exalted. And at
some time, each of us has thought that if we are exalted
in some way, it must mean we are exalting ourselves.
Well, we *could* be exalting ourselves, but the Bible says
that if we humble ourselves under the mighty hand of
God, *He* will exalt us.

God Will Lift You Up

God planned a good life for you before the foundation of the world. His plan is to exalt your life. He
plans to lift you up and make your life better.

Ephesians 1:3 and 4 says, *"Blessed be the God and
Father of our Lord Jesus Christ, who hath blessed us
with all spiritual blessings in heavenly places in
Christ: According as he hath chosen us in him before
the foundation of the world . . . ."* God provided everything we need to break loose from the cares of life.

Now let's look again at First Peter 5:6: *"Humble
yourselves therefore under the mighty hand of God, that
he may exalt you IN DUE TIME."* Notice that God will

exalt you in due time. That means your rising above the cares of life is a process. It will take time. When you humble yourself, He immediately sets into motion the process of exalting you. But you must stay humble under the mighty hand of God to allow the process to lead you to that place where God wants to take you.

Your Part

In the next verse, Peter tells you how to remain humble under God's mighty hand. Verse 7 says you can be humble before God by "casting all your care on Him, for He cares for you." Before you can successfully cast your cares on Him, you have to know that God loves you. That's why the devil sits on your shoulder saying, "How can God love *you*? Don't you know what you have done? Don't you know how you have acted? How in the world can God love you?"

When the devil tells you that, take hold of his head, twist it around, and point it toward Calvary. Tell him, "Mr. Devil, I want you to get a view of Calvary. I want you to get a view of the crucified Lord and Savior Who gave His life and shed His blood to take my place, becoming sin and sickness for *me*. He was pushed away from the Presence of God for *me*, and He, Who knew no sin, was made to be sin for me that I might be made the righteousness of God in Christ Jesus!" (*See* Isa. 53:4–6; 2 Cor. 5:21.)

And if you ever want to know if God cares about you, turn your head and look to Calvary, because it expresses the love of Almighty God. It expresses the extreme degree of God's love toward you. He came and robed Himself in flesh and took your place on Calvary's Cross, setting you free from the curse of the law and making you righteous. Let's look at what Paul stated in his letters to the churches at Galatia and Corinth.

GALATIANS 3:13,14

13 **Christ hath redeemed us from the curse of the law, being made a curse for us: for it is written, Cursed is every one that hangeth on a tree:**

14 **That the blessing of Abraham might come on the Gentiles through Jesus Christ; that we might receive the promise of the Spirit through faith.**

2 CORINTHIANS 5:21

21 **For he hath made him to be sin for us, who knew no sin; that we might be made the righteousness of God in him.**

These verses show us that through Jesus, God draws us unto Himself and presents us holy—without blame and without reproof—in His sight. That, my friend, is the real story of Mount Calvary.

Notify Your Face

You receive the benefits of Calvary by casting all your care on the Lord and allowing Him to care for you. But sometimes you need to notify your face that you have cast your care on Him. Put a joyful look on your face. Now you may say, "I don't feel joyful." Maybe not, but you can at least change the look on your face. Put a joyful expression on your face and say, "I have cast all of my care over on the Lord. Once and for all, I have cast my care, and now I'm going to smile and be joyful. Now I'm going to rejoice; I'm going to give praise and thanks to God. I'm going to do what the Scripture teaches me to do. I'm going to have the mind of the Spirit. I will have life and peace."

The Amplified Bible gives a little different insight into our reference scripture.

1 PETER 5:6,7

6   Therefore humble yourselves [demote, lower yourselves in your own estimation] under the mighty hand of God, that in due time He may exalt you,

7   Casting the whole of your care [all your anxieties, all your worries, all your concerns, once and for all] on Him, for He cares for you affectionately and cares about you watchfully.

Verse 6 is not talking about thinking less of ourselves than we should think. Neither is it talking about thinking more highly of ourselves than we should think. Instead, it tells us not to think for one minute that we can handle the cares of life by ourselves.

If your estimation of yourself is that you can handle your cares on your own, then demote yourself, or lower yourself under the mighty hand of God and say, "God, You and You alone can handle the cares in my life." Humble yourself—demote yourself in your own estimation—under the mighty hand of God so that, in due time, He may exalt you. Cast the whole of your care—all your anxieties, all your worries, all your concerns, once and for all—on Him. Why? Because He cares for you.

Not one sparrow drops to the ground without God taking notice of it. And much more than that, God is watching you so closely that He knows how many hairs you have on your head today.

MATTHEW 10:29–31

29 Are not two sparrows sold for a farthing? and one of them shall not fall on the ground without your Father.

30 But the very hairs of your head are all numbered.

31 Fear ye not therefore, ye are of more value than many sparrows.

Are you not much better than the birds? Are you not much better than the sparrows? Are you not much better than *all* of creation? Yes! You are the apple of God's eye. You are God's prized possession. You are the redeemed of the Lord. And the Scripture says, *"Let the redeemed of the Lord say so"* (Ps. 107:2).

So . . . *say so!*

Some people have let the cares of life rob them of their joy. They have been beaten down with the cares of life. If that is you, then today is the day to get them off you. Cast them away from you, once and for all. Say, "Father, I refuse to touch them again in my thought life. When thoughts of the cares of life come to me, I will not entertain those thoughts."

Now make a full effort to stay in joy, for the joy of the Lord is your strength! And . . . remember to notify your face!

You Shall Not Be Moved!

When you came into Christ through the New Birth—when you were born again and the Spirit of God came to live inside you—you became the righteousness of God. That happened, not because you acted righteous or did anything righteous, but because *Jesus* did something to make you righteous.

Righteous means you are in right standing with God. It is something God, by His own will, decided that He would make you. He wanted to, and did, place you in right standing with Himself through Jesus Christ.

Because of that, He has made you a promise. Psalm 55:22 is talking to you when it says, *"Cast thy burden upon the Lord, and he shall sustain thee: he shall never suffer the righteous to be moved."* Say that verse out loud, but this time put your name in it like this: "I, [insert your name], cast my burden upon the

Lord, and He shall sustain me. He shall never allow [insert your name], the righteous, to be moved."

When we do this, we are repeating what God said in His Word. If He hadn't meant it, He would not have said it. So, since He *did* say it, then we should take Him up on it.

If you will let Him, God will take all of your cares. And He will sustain you so that you will not be moved off your faith.

God does not bring the cares of life to you, nor does He bring the cares of life upon you. God brings *His Word* to you, and He wants His Word in you, renewing the spirit of your mind. Remember, the cares of life are not designed to make you stronger or more spiritual. If anything, they are designed by Satan to *prove* or *test* your spirituality.

Avoid the Chokehold

Two biblical definitions of the word *care* are "to be drawn in different directions" and "division, distraction, worry, and anxiety." From these definitions, we can see that when the cares of life come to you, they bring the potential to cause you to be indecisive, distracted, worried, and anxious—just the opposite of being fixed and immovable.

The cares of life are designed to steal the operative Word of God away from you. They are designed to remove your focus from the Word of God and to get you away from the one thing that will produce fruit in your life.

Satan is after the Word. If you have the Word in your life, he will come and steal it. And if you *don't* have the Word, he will come because he knows you are easy prey. Refuse to move off the Word no matter how difficult the pressures of life may be. God will sustain you.

Another Bible definition of care is "to be double-minded." The Book of James gives us insight about that.

JAMES 1:5–8

5 If any of you lack wisdom, let him ask of God, that giveth to all men liberally, and upbraideth not; and it shall be given him.

6 But let him ask in faith, nothing wavering. For he that wavereth is like a wave of the sea driven with the wind and tossed.

7 For let not that man think that he shall receive any thing of the Lord.

8 A double minded man is unstable in all his ways.

Referring to our definitions of care, we can see that cares cause us to be drawn in two directions. When that happens, we have departed from God and are in a state of unbelief—or double-minded.

Hebrews 3:12 teaches us more about unbelief: *"Take heed, brethren, lest there be in any of you an evil heart of unbelief, in departing from the living God."*

When the cares of life have distracted your mind, divided your thinking, and moved you away from God into an area of double-mindedness, you have moved out of a place of faith. Instead, when that happens, you have come into an area of what the writer of Hebrews calls *a place of evil.* That can happen when you know God is *able* to meet your needs, yet your mind won't let you believe He *will* meet them.

How do you know if you are in that place? You are in that place if your faith is strong when you get up in the morning because everything looks good; then at noon, if anything has worsened, your faith is gone. You are wavering back and forth and you really don't know what you need to do.

Now I am not saying *you* are evil; I'm saying, as the Bible says, what has come to you is causing an evil heart of unbelief. The Bible calls unbelief evil because it opposes God's Word.

Satan's mission is to cause us not to operate in agreement with the oracles of God. He is an enemy of God, and he wants to cause everyone to walk in a place of opposing Him. It is easy to see why demonic forces come to us and launch the cares of life at us. They do it because the cares of life oppose God.

Cares keep the vehicle of faith, which is the Word of God, from coming into your mind and going into your spirit so your words and actions will agree with God. Satan tries to move you off your faith in God because faith pleases God, and Satan doesn't want you to please God. He tries to see to it that you will not receive from God those things that God says in His Word are yours.

If you allow them to, the cares of life will get a chokehold on your spiritual mind. If you leave your mind unattended, allowing fear and cares to do what they are sent to do, God's promises will not come to pass. All the while, you might be saying, "I believe the Word of God." You might even be feeling good about going to a Word church or some other Spirit-filled church, or that your church is spiritually alive. Nevertheless, nothing in your life will change until you receive different information from the Word and then put that information between your ears. Then you must develop the information between your ears so that the spirit of your mind is renewed and your every thought and action is pervaded with the Word of God.

Every time you arrest a thought and examine it until you know whether it agrees with the Word, you are becoming a more spiritually-minded person. You are seeing to it that your actions align themselves with the Word of God. Your spiritual mind will cause you to grab hold of those things that keep you in a place that leads to life and peace.

Guard Your Sense Gates

Cares are introduced to your mind through the sense gates—seeing, feeling, and hearing. If you couldn't see, hear, or feel, you probably would not have a care today.

Satan has access to your hearing, seeing, and feeling senses, and he works in this sense realm to introduce thoughts to your mind. Our faith in God must become *detached* and *separated* from our senses so that the cares of life no longer have any influence on our faith. Ultimately and ideally, only the Word of God should have influence on what we think and believe.

Many people base their faith on what they feel, see, and hear. Then, in addition to using their physical senses, they inject common sense. Common sense is good when used in the right way, but common sense should never replace the Word of God.

If you choose to put the Word of God in your mind, you can erase the "doubt tape" from years past. You can replace that tape regarding the words of doubt with the infallible, indestructible, unfailing Word of the Living God. Then when the cares of life come to the battleground of your mind to wage war, your faith will rise up and say, "If you've come for a fight, then you have a fight on your hands." Faith will win the battle every time and cause the cares of life to depart from your thinking.

Faith—The Rightful Place

L et's recap what we have said so far. When care comes to your life, it can cause you to be drawn in different directions in your thoughts. Care can cause you to be indecisive, and it creates divisions and distractions in your life. Many times, fear introduces cares into your life, causing worry, anxiety, and stress. Taking on the cares of life can be the same as being double-minded. And being double-minded is the same as being without faith, which results in tying God's hands and preventing Him from helping you.

If we find ourselves in this place, James 1:5 says, *"If any of you lack wisdom, let him ask of God, that giveth to all men liberally, and upbraideth not; and it shall be given him."* James goes on to say that without the wisdom of God, we will be unstable.

The word *unstable* means that a person is not set in his or her place. If you are distracted in your mind by the cares of life—be they lack of finances, difficult family relationships, or any other distress—you are allowing those cares to take you out of your *rightful place*. I'm not talking about ministry places or ministry gifts. The rightful place for the children of God *is the place of faith*.

Paul in his writings says the just (or the righteous) shall live by faith (Rom. 1:17; Gal. 3:11). And the Book of Hebrews tells us that faith must be a vital part of our Christian life. Hebrews 11:6 says, *"But without faith it is impossible to please him: for he that cometh to God must believe that he is, and that he is a rewarder of them that diligently seek him."*

An Open Place of Victory

Let's also take note again that cares are *not* designed to mature us, though we need to be mature in the way we handle them; nor are cares designed to make us stronger, though we do need to be strong in dealing with them. Neither are the cares of life designed to develop our character, though we do need to have strong moral fiber while we are handling them. The cares of this world are designed to stop the productivity of the Word of God in our life. They will steal the power of the Word from our life and keep the hand of God from working on our behalf to bring us out in that open place of victory that God's Word says is ours.

Expect God's Power

Cares begin with a troubled state of mind. Satan will introduce negative, doubtful thoughts to you and try to have them remain in your thinking for an extended time without your doing something about them. He is trying to bring you into a place where those thoughts begin to trouble you. That's when worry and anxiety step in.

Worry is "tormenting oneself with disturbing thoughts." Simply stated, worry is torment. (Any worrier knows that!) _Anxiety_ is distress or uneasiness of mind caused by fear of danger or misfortune. Some people get up troubled every morning, expecting the worst to happen. They get up _expecting_ their day not to go right. They say to themselves, "What will happen today? Why, look at yesterday!" They get up expecting something negative to happen. But we should get out of the bed every day expecting God's power to make a difference in our life!

Expect the power of God to be with you no matter what your circumstance, situation, or difficulty. You should expect God's power in your words and actions to cause every situation of your life to bow its knee to the Lordship of Jesus Christ. It doesn't matter what happened yesterday. This is the day the Lord has made, and He wants you to rejoice and be glad in it (Ps. 118:24). His mercies and faithfulness are new every morning (Lam. 3:21–23). This is a new day and a new time and we should refuse to be captured by what happened yesterday. We should be moved only by what we know can happen today in God.

(A certain energy comes from a troubled mind, just as an energy comes from a mind of faith; but the energies are poles apart. One type is negative energy from the enemy; the other is positive energy from God.)

Guard Your Mind and Your Mouth

Satan is after your mind. If he can get your mind, he has *you*. If he can control your thoughts, he can control you. Even if he attacks your body, your finances, or your family, he is after your mind.

Satan wants to negatively disturb or interfere with your body's normal physiological equilibrium, which includes the mental and emotional balance of your life. He seeks to get you out of balance in your mind with the cares of life. He wants you out of balance, falling away from faith, the Word, and all God wants for you.

What is Satan trying to do? He is trying to get to and destroy the things in your life that will bear good fruit. He is trying to steal the good things from your life. When he comes to you with thoughts of fear, pain, worry, and other negative influences, and tries to affect your emotional and physical balance, he is trying to come in to take the Word out of your mind. He wants to negate, or reduce to zero, the effectiveness of the Word of God in your life.

When our thoughts become negative, those thoughts are denying God. You might be thinking, _Oh, I never deny God_; yet you will entertain doubt in your mind, which is a form of denial because doubtful thoughts are contrary to His Word. You are supposed to bring that doubt-filled thought into subjection to the Word.

If you let doubtful thoughts linger in your mind, the next thing you know, they will transfer from your mind to your tongue. Why? Because you chose not to deal with what Satan introduced and now it has captured your mind.

Negative thoughts left in the mind will produce words that expressly deny the Word of God. These might be words such as, "God has not met my need yet," "God has not healed me yet," and "God hasn't answered my prayer yet."

The following scriptures prove that these are words of denial. Philippians 4:19 says, _"But my God shall supply all your need according to his riches in glory by Christ Jesus."_ First Peter 2:24 says, _"Who his own self bare our sins in his own body on the tree, that we, being dead to sins, should live unto righteousness: by whose stripes ye were healed."_ And First John 5:14 and 15 says, _"And this is the confidence that we have in him,_ *that, if we ask any thing according to his will, he heareth us: And if we know that he hear us, whatsoever we ask, we know that we have the petitions that we desired of him."*

Still, thoughts come to us such as: *God hasn't done that for me, has he?* If we meditate on such thoughts about healing, the next thought will be to "feel and see" or "look and see" if we are healed. All of this is how we begin denying God and His Word.

No Spiritual 'Roundup'

Sometimes we let negative thoughts run rampant in our mind, and then we come to church and try to have them washed out with one sermon. That won't work.

When negative thoughts are allowed to remain in the mind, the normal response is to speak those words. Then the words of doubt are not only words of denial in your mind; they have become the confession of your mouth. If you speak them out, sooner or later you will have to deal with them.

It's a spiritual principle that words are seeds. Luke 8:11 says, *"Now the parable is this: The seed is the word of God."*

Some people think they can say what they want to and then just pick up a bottle of "spiritual Roundup" and kill all of the sprouts coming from the bad seed they planted. (Roundup is a brand of weed killer.) They pray, "Kill all those bad seeds, Lord," or, "Lord, I just pray for Roundup." Soon, the little seedlings they missed with the Roundup begin growing, and suddenly they begin wondering, "What is going on Lord? Why is this happening in my life?" It can't necessarily be traced back to yesterday or last week, but somewhere way back down the line, maybe even years ago, they sowed the seed. Now suddenly that little seed shoots up, and they are dumbfounded. But that plant is growing because they didn't deal with the little bad seeds before they planted them along the way.

The confession of our mouth is supposed to be aligned with the Word of God. When we speak His Word out of our mouth from a heart of faith, God watches over it to perform it. And all of Heaven cooperates to see to it that it comes to pass.

God said we were healed, so speak it! God said we are prosperous, so speak it! To do otherwise is to deny the integrity of God's Word.

The Rudder of Life

If you speak words contrary to the Word of God, they are words of doubt. When thoughts that bring cares to your life are left in your mind, you will transfer them to your tongue or lips as words. When that happens, you have put those negative words upon the rudder of your life, the very thing that gives your life direction. Unfortunately, you have turned that rudder in the wrong direction with those negative words.

The Book of James tells us about this rudder.

JAMES 3:3–5

3   **Behold, we put bits in the horses' mouths, that they may obey us; and we turn about their whole body.**

4   **Behold also the ships, which though they be so great, and are driven of fierce winds, yet are they turned about with a very small helm, whithersoever the governor listeth.**

5   **Even so the tongue is a little member, and boasteth great things. Behold, how great a matter a little fire kindleth!**

Notice that James says these ships are driven of, or by, fierce winds. Yet a tiny rudder makes a huge ship turn wherever the pilot wants it to go, even though the winds are strong. This verse tells us that a little rudder on the huge ship is greater than the fierce winds. And it tells us we have something at our disposal that is comparable to that rudder—our tongue.

Though the winds may blow and the storms may assail, we have something in our mouth that can point us in the right direction, turning our ship. Those winds can blow and howl, but they can't keep our ship from turning in the right direction in the middle of the storm, if we use our tongue at the right time and in the right way.

Some people wait until a storm has leveled their house, and then they get up and talk about what a mess it is. Don't do that. Use your tongue in the right way before the storm and during the storm, and the "house" of your life will stand fast.

The tongue is a small thing, but what enormous damage it can do! A great forest can be set on fire by one tiny spark. Your tongue is to your life as the spark is to the forest fire.

Say What?

It's up to us what our tongue sparks in our life. When we allow our tongue to set our life in motion for defeat, it is because Satan has introduced a thought with a care wrapped in it. He brought that thought to our mind and our mind grabbed hold of it and thought it. Suddenly we are meditating on that thought instead of doing what we are supposed to do, which is casting down imaginations and every high thing that exalts itself against the knowledge of God.

The next thing we are to do when Satan brings a negative thought to our mind is to immediately put the Word of God on the rudder of our life. We must not only meditate on God's Word, but we must _speak_ what His Word says about our situation, what the Holy Spirit is doing, and what the Word says we are to do. Doing all of this causes that negative thought to be cast down so that it does not become a stronghold in our mind.

What are you doing with your tongue? If you are speaking the Word of God, you are turning your ship in the direction you want it to go. You are turning your ship toward deliverance . . . toward power . . . toward praise. In a nutshell, you are turning your ship toward victory.

You can turn your ship toward the Word of God with the words of your mouth. Though the winds may be blowing fiercely on the sea of your life, the little rudder in your mouth—if you keep it pointed in the right direction by the Spirit, the power, and the faith of God—will cause you to overcome. You can come out victorious, no matter how fierce the storm is that assails you.

Faith must be in your heart and in your mouth. Romans 10:8 says, *"But what saith it? The word is nigh thee, even in thy mouth, and in thy heart: that is, the word of faith, which we preach."* So based on the Word of God, put what you need on the rudder. God's Word is your compass; it shows you which way you need to move the rudder. You are to have the *spirit* of faith, not just the formulas of faith.

You can tell when a person really has hold of the spirit of faith. Just watch the rudder—listen to his or her words. You can tell the direction people's rudder is pointed by what they say. The Bible says Abraham acted like God, calling things that be not as though they were (Rom. 4:17). Abraham understood what to put on his rudder to point his ship in the right direction. He spoke the word of faith.

Hebrews 11:1 says, *"Now faith is the substance of things hoped for . . . ."* So we could say that calling those things which be not as though they were is the substance of things hoped for and the evidence of things not seen. Hebrews 11:6 says, *"Without faith it is impossible to please God."* We can also say this: Without calling those things that be not as though they were, it is impossible to please God. These statements would be just as scriptural as using the word *faith*.

You can deal with the cares of life in a productive way. You do it with the rudder of your life. Your tongue is the starting place. Your actions will begin to line up with God's Word when you put the right words in your mouth. When you do that, you will suddenly see your ship turning in the middle of the fierce winds. You can look behind you and see all the mess, but if you just keep using your rudder, you will deal in the right way with the cares of your life. Before long, you will look back and see the trial further away from you, behind you, and after a while longer, you will look back and hardly see it. Then when the next trial presents itself to you, you will be moving away from it long before it can come on board.

Keep in mind: the cares of life are designed to steal the Word out of your life and cause you to be a nonproductive Christian.

6

Be Ready!

It is a known fact that when you decide to get closer to God, trials shoot at you from all sides. But the way you see the tests and trials, and the way you see yourself *in* them, will determine your outcome.

Let's look in the Bible to see an illustration of that:

DANIEL 3:14–16

14 Nebuchadnezzar spake and said unto them, Is it true, O Shadrach, Meshach, and Abednego, do not ye serve my gods, nor worship the golden image which I have set up?

15 Now if ye be ready that at what time ye hear the sound of the cornet, flute, harp, sackbut, psaltery, and dulcimer, and all kinds of music, ye fall down and worship the image which I have made; well: but if ye

worship not, ye shall be cast the same hour into the midst of a burning fiery furnace; and who is that God that shall deliver you out of my hands?

16 Shadrach, Meshach, and Abednego, answered and said to the king, O Nebuchadnezzar, we are not careful to answer thee in this matter.

Notice the answer they gave: " . . . *O Nebuchadnezzar, we are not careful to answer thee in this matter*" (v. 16). Another Bible translation renders those words as, "We are ready to answer thee in this matter."

A Position of Readiness

All of us should be in a position of readiness to answer when a trial knocks on the door. Don't wait until it knocks on the door and *then* try to get ready. You will find it difficult, if not impossible, to get ready if you wait until the trial knocks on your door. Yet sometimes people do that. When everything is moving along smoothly in their lives, they tend to relax and not do as they would if trouble were knocking. That leaves them unprepared to answer a fiery trial. After it knocks on the door, comes in and lies on the couch, and turns on the TV, they try to get it out of their house. They beat it, discuss it, rebuke it, and fight it—all because they were not ready when it first arrived. Being ready makes a lot of difference, because if they are not ready when the care gets there, they will have more difficulty seeing themselves coming out victoriously.

As we read further in Daniel chapter 3, we see how Shadrach, Meshach, and Abednego answered the king:

DANIEL 3:17,18

17 If it be so, our God whom we serve is able to deliver us from the burning fiery furnace, and he will deliver us out of thine hand, O king.

18 But if not, be it known unto thee, O king, that we will not serve thy gods, nor worship the golden image which thou hast set up.

These three Hebrews saw themselves coming out, not dying in the flames. Isn't that right? They said if the king _did_ throw them in, their God would deliver them. Then they flipped the coin and said if the king _did not_ throw them in, they still would not bow. They answered the king fearlessly.

Contrary to some teaching, the "if not" in verse 18 is not saying "if God _doesn't_ deliver us;" it is saying, "if _you_ [the king] _don't_ throw us in." Many people preach that the three Hebrew boys were saying, "If he throws us in, God will deliver us, but if God doesn't deliver us . . . . If the latter were true, that would be double-minded, wouldn't it? If that had been their attitude, they would not have survived being thrown into that furnace. With that attitude, they would have had no faith in God to bring them out in victory. And without faith in God, they would have burned up just as the soldiers did who threw them into the fiery furnace. But their confidence was in God, and their courageous statement meant that they would not compromise in that test and trial.

Don't See the Flames

The three Hebrew boys seemed to be between a rock and a hard place . . . but that was not really the way it was for them. They gave us a good example to follow when the king asked, " . . . *and who is that God that shall deliver you out of my hands?*"

When that happened, the boys didn't talk to each other, questioning their faith in God, saying, "I wonder if God is going to do it. What if the Lord doesn't come through?"

Sometimes you may find yourself between a rock and a hard place. This sort of thought will come to you, telling you to doubt your God. Just remember, it's just the devil, trying to silence you in your faith.

The Hebrew boys had no doubt. They not only believed God was able to deliver them, but they believed God *would* deliver them. Believing God is able is vastly different from believing He *will*.

These Hebrew boys stood up to King Nebuchadnezzar and said, in a sense, "King, we have no care about this situation. If you throw us in there, first, the God we serve is able, and second, we announce to you that He *will* deliver us. So go ahead, King, and put us in there. Tie us up and throw us in, but we are going to show you our God."

When the threat came from their king, they saw their God; they didn't see the flames. The flames took the lives of the men who threw them in, but the boys didn't see the flames and did not feel the heat. They looked at the situation from both ends. If they were thrown in, they had made up their mind from the beginning what they would not do—they would not worship the idols and they would not let it become a care in their mind.

Crispy Critters?

Shadrach, Meshach, and Abednego knew the king had signed a decree that everyone had to bow down and worship the image of the king. Those who didn't do it would be punished, but in their mind they saw their God delivering them—they never thought once that He would not deliver them.

Let me ask you a question: If you didn't do what someone told you to do and a furnace, seven times hotter than normal, was waiting for you, what would you think? Some people would think, I'm a crispy critter . . .

Wouldn't that be a normal thought? The furnace is seven times hotter than usual, so wouldn't it be expected, in the natural, to think that if you were to go into that furnace you would be on your way to becoming a "crispy critter"?

Has the devil ever told you he was going to make you a crispy critter? He may not have threatened you in those exact words, but I am sure he has threatened you.

In contrast to the Hebrew boys' not bowing to the king's image, when we let care occupy our mind, we have bowed our knee to the image that Satan has brought to our life to get us out of position. We will have many opportunities to bow to his images, but we must refuse to do it.

Say this to yourself: "I refuse to bow to Satan's image. I will be in God's position and place for me. I will be at my post of duty, full of the Holy Ghost, full of power, and full of tenacity and zeal. I will do it."

When the opportunity for care presents itself, what you see will determine your outcome. You can come out of the trial a crispy critter, or you can come out victorious. It's up to you.

When the three Hebrew boys came out of the furnace and their clothes weren't burned, their hair was not singed, and there was no smell of smoke on them. They went through hell and came out without the smell of hell on them. If you are catching hell, don't hold it. If you are walking through hell, don't stop. If you are under the attacks of hell, you should launch a counterattack from the Word of God to defeat the care that is trying to overwhelm you.

Don't Think It's Strange

Sometimes when people encounter tests and trials, they come to me and ask, "Brother Charles, can you tell me what I've done wrong?" The truth is, no, I can't. I can't tell them what they have done wrong unless they do it while they are standing in front of me. They ask because they are dealing with a trial in their life and they are thinking, _What have I done? Why has this thing come to me?_

It seems they think if they can pinpoint something they have done wrong and then fix it, then whatever is coming against their life will just leave. However, notice what the Word of God says about that in First Peter 4:12: _"Beloved, think it not strange concerning the fiery trial which is to try you, as though some strange thing happened unto you."_

We can see from this statement that if we are breathing, we will have trials. First, Peter tells us in this verse, "Don't think it strange." In other words, don't be dumbfounded by it. Don't be thrown off guard by it. Then he says clearly that the fiery trial is to try you.

The Book of Mark further explains why we should not be surprised when trials come:

MARK 4:14–17

14 **The sower soweth the word.**

15 **And these are they by the way side, where the word is sown; but when they have**

> heard, Satan cometh immediately, and
> taketh away the word that was sown in
> their hearts.
>
> 16 And these are they likewise which are sown
> on stony ground; who, when they have
> heard the word, immediately receive it
> with gladness;
>
> 17 And have no root in themselves, and so
> endure but for a time: afterward, when
> affliction or persecution ariseth FOR THE
> WORD'S SAKE, immediately they are
> offended.

Do you see in this passage *why* affliction and perse-cution come? The Bible says they arise for the Word's sake. In other words, when you hear the Word, Satan comes with persecution and affliction to try to steal the Word before it can take root and become firmly estab-lished in your heart.

The enemy wants nothing more than to see us dis-believing God's Word.

Don't Be a Laughing Abraham

Abraham, a patriarch of old, is mentioned many times throughout the Scriptures. In the New Testament, we are told we are heirs of faithful Abraham. We are also told that we are heirs of the blessings of Abraham. We appropriate these blessing by faith, so let's look at the life of Abraham, who is called the father of faith, so we can better understand faith principles.

First, we know that God is our Father, but we know that Abraham became known as the father of faith because he first introduced what believing God really is. Let's read how this journey of faith began.

GENESIS 17:15–22

15 And God said unto Abraham, As for Sarai thy wife, thou shalt not call her name Sarai, but Sarah shall her name be.

16 And I will bless her, and give thee a son also of her: yea, I will bless her, and she shall be a mother of nations; kings of people shall be of her.

17 Then Abraham fell upon his face, and laughed, and said in his heart, Shall a child be born unto him that is a hundred years old? and shall Sarah, that is ninety years old, bear?

18 And Abraham said unto God, O that Ishmael might live before thee!

19 And God said, Sarah thy wife shall bear thee a son indeed; and thou shalt call his name Isaac: and I will establish my covenant with him for an everlasting covenant, and with his seed after him.

20 And as for Ishmael, I have heard thee: Behold, I have blessed him, and will make him fruitful, and will multiply him exceedingly; twelve princes shall he beget, and I will make him a great nation.

21 But my covenant will I establish with Isaac, which Sarah shall bear unto thee at this set time in the next year.

22 And he left off talking with him, and God went up from Abraham.

When Abraham heard God's promise to give him Isaac, through whom God promised to make Abraham the father of many nations, Abraham fell on his face and laughed.

Isn't that what we do sometimes? Too often, we hear about the abundant blessings God wants to give us and we laugh, thinking it could never happen. At times, as I preach the Word, I can almost hear people's mind when I tell them about their inheritance of the blessings of God. I can almost hear them think, *You have to be kidding!*

If people think like that, it is no different from what Abraham did; it is the same as falling on their face and laughing. The Bible says he fell on his face and laughed, saying the wrong things in his heart (the word used in the original Hebrew also means "mind").

When God's Word first came to Abraham, the first thing he had to do was deal with it between his ears. Immediately, he questioned the word of the Lord. He asked, *"Shall a child be born unto him that is a hundred years old?"* (v. 17). It is almost as if he asked, "God, have you checked our birth certificates lately?"

What was Abraham doing here? He was dealing with his mind.

Don't Take the Care

When God's Word comes to you, right alongside it can come an opportunity for you to take a care. The Word itself doesn't bring the care; but how you _deal_ with the Word that comes to you can introduce an opportunity to take a care. Abraham was leaving himself wide open for taking on the care of what God had spoken. He said, "I'm a hundred years old. Shall a child be born unto him that is a hundred years old? Shall Sarah who is 90 years old bear?" Though Abraham wanted to please God, he thought he was incapable of doing what God said.

Dealing with the word from God this way caused Abraham to look at himself and his wife. He didn't see much promise in the natural. After years of not conceiving with Sarah, he had already turned to Sarah's servant Hagar and had a son, Ishmael, with her.

Ishmael was 13 years old when Abraham said to God, _"Oh that Ishmael might live before thee."_ What was happening here? Abraham thought he had a better idea—to become the father of many nations through Ishmael instead of believing God's promise and waiting for Isaac.

Have you ever tried to convince God you had a better idea, a plan you thought would work better than what He had planned for you? If so, you are just like Abraham. He was dealing with his mind and thoughts. He was dealing with what you and I have to deal with when the Word is preached, or when the Word of the Lord comes to us in our spirit, saying something so good or so big that it is hard for us to believe. How we handle what He says, though, will determine whether we get our "Isaac" or not.

God told Abraham He would give him a son through Sarah. He said, *"I will bless her and she shall be a mother of nations."* Here God stated to Abraham what He was going to do. God's will was fixed and settled, but Abraham had to deal with it in his mind.

God Is Not Holding Out

How you handle the urge toward unbelief will determine whether you get what you need in your life. How you handle that urge will determine whether the promises of God will come into your life and manifest *in power*. God is not holding out on you. Only you can short-circuit His blessings in your life.

Now each of us needs to ask, "What am I going to do with what God says?" Like Abraham, we have to move beyond "myself, my wife, my Ishmael"—which could be anything we lean on that feeds our unbelief and is different from what God's Word says is ours. We need to say, "I have to move beyond my own carnal thinking and get something going in my life based on God's Word."

If what you are doing is not working today, stand up in faith and get something else going in your life. You need to push all the junk out of your life and get the Word inside you and let it begin to work for you.

The Spirit of Faith

As it is written, I have made thee a father of many nations,) before him whom he believed, even God, who quickeneth the dead, and calleth those things which be not as though they were.

—Romans 4:17

Think about that verse for a minute. God calls those things that be not as though they were. (We want to call things that are, or might be, as though they are.)

But I want you to see that Paul says in this verse that Abraham had acted like God. The Bible says God calls those things which be not as though they were, and Abraham began to do the same, just like God had done.

God wants us to have that same spirit of faith. Paul, in one of his Corinthian letters, says, *"We having the same spirit of faith, according as it is written, I*

*believed, and therefore have I spoken; we also believe,
and therefore speak"* (2 Cor. 4:13). This is talking about
having that same spirit of faith—believing what is
written in the Word and saying it.

Faith shouldn't be some formula that you grab off
the shelf when the trials and tests of life come. Faith
needs to be the spirit about your life that shows up in
your words. You should have such a spirit of faith
about you that when you get up in the morning, everything looks rosy and bright around you. You should
have a spirit of faith that says, "God is God this morning." Or if you get up and the clouds happen to be over
your head, you should have that spirit of faith that
says, "The same God who was with me when the sun
was shining is with me now. These clouds and storms
must go. This storm must pass. These cares have to get
out of my mind—they can't stay—for I have the same
spirit of faith that my God has. And I will call those
things that be not as though they were. I choose to be
a person of faith."

Abraham did something like that when he rose up
off the ground. Something happened that changed him.
It not only changed his life and his family but, because
of his faithfulness, it also changed the destiny of every
person in the Kingdom of God today. Abraham changed
our destiny when he rose up off the ground, fixed his
mind in the right direction, and decided he would be a
man of faith.

Calling those things that be not as though they were, Abraham was the one *"who against hope believed in hope, that he might become the father of many nations, according to that which was spoken . . ."* (Rom. 4:18).

Already Blessed

We can become what God wants us to be only according to that which He has spoken. We will not get there any other way. If we don't get there according to what He spoke, we will not get there. Crying, pity parties, bickering, arguing, complaining, and having divided minds will not get us where we need to be. We will become what God already says we are when we take His Word from the pages of His Book, put it in our heart, and allow it to erase the old doubt tapes in our mind that have dominated our thinking, speaking, and acting.

After those old tapes have been erased and new tapes of the Word of God are dominating our thinking, speaking, and acting, the winds still will blow, and the storms still will come. The wolf still will howl, but we will stand and say, "Not in my house you don't! You will not come up on my front porch and howl like that. I'll knock you across the street!"

God always refers to His blessings in the past tense. When we come to the place in our thinking where we begin to see them that way—where we see that the promises of God are already ours—we will move into the same spirit of faith that God has.)If we don't come to that place in our thinking, we will always live in nothing more than hope—always looking to the future, but rarely seeing any fruit from the promises of God.

The Oracles of God

First Peter 4:11 and 12 says, *"If any man speak, let him speak as the oracles of God; if any man minister, let him do it as of the ability which God giveth: that God in all things may be glorified . . . ."*

Notice that Peter said: ". . . that God in all things may be glorified." He is telling us to glorify God in our speech. We know that God is not glorified when we fill our words with doubt and unbelief, fear, and uncertainty. We know that God is not pleased with that. Sometimes people think that filling their words with fear and uncertainty shows some kind of humility before God. They think it shows God that they are not trusting in themselves and they are not able to deal with their situation by themselves.

But remember, humbling ourselves before God shows that we *do* understand that we can't handle our situations by ourselves. As we look to Him and fill our words with His sayings, we show Him that we believe His Word above our troubles and we believe He is faithful to perform that Word.

The Bible says Abraham "... *against hope believed in hope, that he might become the father of many nations, according to that which was spoken . . ."* (Rom. 4:18). The only way we will become what God tells us we are is to get hold of this. We must make up our mind that we will act on what He said, and we must speak the oracles of God. We must say what God said.

First Peter 4:11 says *"if any man speak, let him speak as the oracles of God."* Here Peter is not talking specifically about preaching; he is talking about saying what God says. If you speak the oracles of God, you can have the same spirit of faith He has. The oracles of God are the sayings, or utterances, of God—so if any man speaks, let him speak in line with the sayings or utterances of God.

We must do that even when our circumstances seem impossible and the situation seems to be *anything but* what God's Word says.

At first, Abraham must have thought his situation was too difficult for God to handle. He must have thought, *God, let's not make this too hard. Sarah and I can't have a baby, but Ishmael is already alive.*

I don't know about you, but sometimes I, too, think my situation is too difficult for God. At times I think, *By the way, God, have You looked at me lately? I know You parted the Red Sea and I know You took the children of Israel across the Jordan. I know You sent quail to them, and manna from Heaven. I know You were with Daniel in the den of lions, and You were with the three Hebrew children in the fiery furnace. You have done miracles before, but have You looked at me? Lord, have You considered Your servant? Lord, have You considered my circumstances lately?*

Sometimes, we try to convince God to look at our circumstances. But He knows all about them, and He is not discouraged by any of them. Furthermore, He doesn't want us to be discouraged. He wants us *to live by faith in Him*—never forgetting that He is the God of the impossible.

How can you tell if you are in faith? Faith always has a good report. Faith always has a praise. Faith always has a song. And that song is not of doom, gloom, and despair. Faith always has a song of victory, of being a winner—an overcomer, more than a conqueror—a song that says, "No weapon formed against me shall prosper. Every tongue that rises against me in judgment, I shall condemn" (Isa. 54:17). Faith always has a song that says, "Mountain, get out of my way; I'm taking you to the sea!" Faith always has a song and always has a praise. It always has a victory report. It always has something good to say about the blessings of God. Faith will rejoice in whatever it is you are believing God for.

This kind of faith is only found in giving our mind over to continually hearing the Word of God. Romans 10:17 says, *"So then faith cometh by hearing, and hearing by the word of God."*

If we hear the Word of God when we come to church but never open, read, meditate, or speak the Word for ourselves any other time, then the spirit of our mind is not renewed and we can't have a spirit of faith. We are at the mercy of circumstances, and cares have a wide-open door to enter through. Because our mind is not renewed, we will receive a care. And that care will bring division, distraction, worry, and anxiety, which in turn will bring stress into our life and rob us of any faith we might have had.

Now we don't read, study, and speak the Word of God just for information. If we are doing it for information only, we are just _religious_, not empowered to overcome cares by our faith. We must allow the Word of God to renew the spirit of our mind.

A Renewed Mind

Renewing the spirit of your mind not only puts the power of the Word in your mind; it also puts it into your actions. Whatever you put in your mind, your actions will follow.

When you became a Christian, your spirit was born of God. So if you are hearing what is in your spirit, you are hearing the voice of the Holy Spirit from within your spirit; or you are hearing the Voice of God out of your spirit. Either way, the message coming from your spirit must be filtered through your mind before you can act on it. It must come up from inside you through your mind. If the Word is not on the tape in your mind when the voice of the Spirit tries to come up, the mind says, "Reject . . . reject." Your mind pushes the reject button and does not want to accept it.

On the other hand, if the spirit of your mind has been renewed to the Word, when the voice of the Spirit comes to your mind, your mind will agree with it and hook up with the Word. Then you will have Bible wisdom to handle the cares of your life.

You choose what to allow in your mind. When your mind goes into action, whatever is on the tape in your mind will play and become your predominant way of thinking. Once care is introduced to you, it will push that play button and, suddenly, thoughts will flood your mind.

If the spirit of your mind has not been renewed, then you will begin to hear something like, *Oh my, I'm going down this time.* Or maybe you'll hear, *Oh my goodness, what am I going to do?* Once that message begins to play in your mind, if you leave it in your mind and don't deal with it, the care will take hold of your mind and bring stress to your life. You will become deeply *stressed out* over the situation. You may even end up at the doctor's office getting a prescription for anti-anxiety or anti-depression medication.

You may be thinking, *I'm taking that kind of medication. Should I feel condemned?* No, you shouldn't feel condemned, but you should be getting hold of the spiritual principles in this book. Now don't get offended and think, *He is really getting on my case because I'm taking medicine.* I'm not. And I'm not telling you not to take your medicine. I'm saying God's Word and His healing power are available to you.

I take an aspirin occasionally myself, but medication can keep you on the negative side of the coin. If you want to approach your situation from the negative side of the coin, that's your business. But I choose to get over on the positive side of the coin. When I'm doing that, praise God, His Word is helping me!

No Negative Side Effects

Unlike prescription drugs, God's Word will give a lasting effect, with no negative side effects. God's Word will not give you bleeding ulcers in the stomach; when taken as prescribed, it will bring health and healing from the top of your head to the soles of your feet. You can be on your way to health and healing and wholeness and wellness in your life if you will decide, *I am going to get the tape right.*

When stress is so heavy on your life that it begins to affect your physical body, you might ask people to pray for your healing, but God can't heal you. That doesn't mean God doesn't have the power to heal you. God has power to do anything He wants to do. But as long as stress remains in your life, even if God does heal you, the problems in your body will come back by next Monday.

God could touch your life with healing, but when the symptoms come back to you because of stress, the doubt tape in your mind would begin playing again: *"Well, I THOUGHT I got healed. I really FELT like I was healed in that service the other morning."* And as you entertain these doubting thoughts, you allow symptoms to bring the care back into your life.

God can't do things for some people. Why? Because they won't let Him. I repeat: *they won't let Him.*

What About Common Sense?

Sometimes we look at the promises of God and they contradict everything we see in the natural. If we are not careful, we will let what we call *common sense* wash the sense of God right out of our mind. Abraham's age, his wife's age, and a son already born were his immediate common-sense responses to the voice of God. And we respond the same way today. Let me give you an example.

If you are not a tither, and suddenly the Spirit of the Lord speaks to your heart to become a tither, you will first have to deal with your mind. When God speaks to you about finances, your mind gets involved. Your mind causes you to say, "I don't have enough. Have you seen my checkbook lately?"

Your mind will decide whether you rebel or not. But if your mind rebels about tithing, it is because you don't have the Word between your ears about the benefits and responsibility of tithing. You don't have enough of the Word in your mind to wash those rebellious thoughts away.

When you hear God tell you to tithe, the play button of your mind is punched. Immediately, your tape begins to play. You might hear two or three quotes of "greater is He that is in me, than he that is in the world" (*see* 1 John 4:4). Then the tape plays again and you hear, *What if this? What if that? Did you know this? Did you know that? What about what happened before?*

Suddenly, these thoughts and cares are playing on the tape along with the Word, and you forget about the two scriptures that played first.

However, if "greater is He that is in me than he that is in the world" has really been recorded over and over again on the tape in your mind, this tape begins to get louder: *Greater is He that is in me than he that is in the world! Greater is He that is in me than he that is in the world! Greater is He that is in me than he that is in the world!* If that scriptural truth is on your tape, it gets louder and louder until it drowns out the common sense tape. For Abraham, common sense said, *Look at me, look at her, look at Ishmael.* For you, it might be, *Look at my checkbook balance, look at the kids' shoes,* or *look at the bills that are due next week.*

Common sense says, "How can you tithe when you can't even pay your bills?" But the Word of God says tithing will bring supernatural help on the scene to make sure your bills are paid!

When the Word-of-God tape drowns out the common-sense tape, all you will hear in your mind and heart is something like this: *I can do all things through Christ which strengthens me . . . no weapon formed against me shall prosper . . . every tongue that rises against me in judgment, I shall condemn . . . thanks be unto God who always causes me to triumph in Christ Jesus . . . God always gives me the victory through my Lord Jesus Christ!*

That tape will start to play over and over, and get louder and louder, and you will begin to praise out loud. Then the devil will say, "I have to leave! This is hurting my ears. I have to go!"

You can inflict some serious damage on Satan's eardrums with your praise. You can say, "Satan, if you keep trying to bring this into my mind, I'm going to get stronger and stronger. I'll get louder and louder. I'll praise loudly when I'm on my feet and when I'm lying down. I'll praise on my way to work and I'll praise *while* I'm working."

Have you ever heard a loud, sharp sound that seemed to pierce your eardrums? Your praise will do that; it will pierce Satan's eardrums.

The Bible says we are to draw near to God and He will draw near to us. Resist the devil (*see* James 4:7,8).

How can we resist the devil? Stand up and praise God, give Him glory, and say, "Devil, this care that you are trying to introduce to me did not come from God. It didn't come from the Word. It came from out there in the natural, or it came from my own thinking. So I'm going to praise God until that thought is washed out of my mind—until it is gone and returns no more!" When you do this, you have just allowed your "God sense" to replace common sense.

Change Your Thinking

For Abraham to be a man of faith, not to mention the *father* of faith, he had to correct his common-sense response. To deal with the doubt that had come to his mind, Abraham had to consider *Who* had spoken to him.

God said He was going to bless Sarah. She would conceive and bear Abraham a son. From this son, nations would come—people as numerous as the stars of the sky and the grains of sand of the seashore. If Abraham had not dealt with the doubt that came to him, it would have become a care to him and would have stolen the promise God spoke to him—and Isaac never would have come on the scene.

But Abraham did deal with that doubt. He changed his thinking.

Romans 4:17 says, "*(As it is written, I have made thee a father of many nations,) before him whom he believed, even God . . . .*" What is this saying? It's saying God was before Abraham, and Abraham believed the One Who was before him.

This verse goes on to say, *". . . who quickeneth the dead, and calleth those things which be not as though they were."* If you can't call those things that "be not" as though they were, then none of God's Word is on your tape—you have nothing to believe but your circumstances.

Paul wrote in Second Corinthians 4:13: *"We having the same spirit of faith, according as it is written, I believed, and therefore have I spoken; we also believe, and therefore speak."*

That is exactly what Paul was talking about when he said that God was before Abraham. So Abraham, after first falling on the floor laughing, began to do what God does: he began calling things that be not as though they were.

What you really believe will come out of your mouth when you are under pressure. If you are saying what God says in His Word, then you have the key to dealing with the cares of life.

Abraham *Did* Consider His Body

Now let's look at another interesting point about Abraham's dilemma. In the New Testament, Romans 4:19 says, *"And being not weak in faith, he considered not his own body now dead, when he was about an hundred years old, neither yet the deadness of Sara's womb."* However, we know he *did* consider his body—and Sarah's infertile womb.

In the Old Testament, the Bible says Abraham at first took into account how old he was, which means he considered his own body. Then he turned to his wife and considered her body. Still, the New Testament says he *did not* consider his body. So, what is wrong here? Is the Bible wrong? No! The second account just means that Abraham changed and, to God, it was as if he never made the first mistake of considering his circumstances above what He had said!

Abraham turned his thinking around. He must have said to himself, *God spoke to me in Ur, and I'm going to get this right*. Abraham corrected himself and began to say what God said.

At first, Abraham's mind was flooded with thoughts because of the words God spoke to him. He had an opportunity to take on care. He began to look at all the circumstances, which seemed to prove that what God said was wrong. Abraham considered himself, he considered his wife, and he considered Ishmael, his first-born son. But somewhere in the process, he made a quality decision and considered God instead of his circumstances. He made a choice of life, which brought God's power on the scene to rejuvenate the ovaries and all the reproductive processes in Sarah. Everything on the inside of her rejuvenated when Abraham said, "God did it before me, and I'm going to do it just like God: I will call those things that be not as though they are." Then he called to Sarah, "Come in here, Sarah. Come in here *now!*"

When God's Word was introduced to Abraham's mind, Abraham's first response was to doubt and take upon himself care instead of faith. When Abraham changed, the Bible says he ". . . *against hope believed in hope, that he might become the father of many nations, according to that which was spoken, So shall thy seed be. And being not weak in faith, he considered not his own body now dead . . .*" (Rom. 4:18,19).

We must stop considering our natural circumstances and, instead, place our hope and faith in that which has been spoken—the Word of God. If you haven't always done that when the cares of life have come, don't feel condemned and beaten up about it. Just change your way of thinking. Abraham did, and you can too.

Judge God Faithful

Today, we are heirs of the promise and covenant that God gave to faithful Abraham. We should be glad and rejoice that Abraham was faithful to God and that Abraham did what was necessary to keep the covenant binding until Jesus came and fulfilled it.

Somewhere between the account in Genesis and the account in Romans, something happened that caused Abraham to get up off the ground where he lay laughing in doubt and unbelief about what God had said to him. The change brought him to a place where he, indeed, became faithful Abraham, the father of faith. The change came after he considered Who had spoken to him.

Now the word _consider_ in the New Testament means, "to fix your mind upon." So we could say that Abraham had to turn his attention from what he could see in the natural and fix his mind upon the One Who had spoken to him. The promise was fulfilled because He judged God faithful.

We must judge God faithful, for if we don't, our faith can't work. Sarah received strength to conceive because she judged Him faithful Who had promised. We, too, have to renew our mind until we come to the place of believing God's Word because we _know_ He is faithful.

If God says something in His Word, it's exactly what He means, and it is exactly what He will do. If God said it, He will do it for me and He will do it for you. We must refuse to allow the cares of life to back us into a corner and attach worry and anxiety to our mind. Instead, we must consider, or fix our mind upon, the faithfulness of God.

God made a covenant with Abraham, the man who would stand in the place of the Lord Jesus Christ until He could make His appearance. The Scripture says, ". . . _When the fulness of time was come, God sent forth his_

Son, made of a woman, made under the law, To redeem them that were under the law . . ." (Gal. 4:4,5). If Abraham had not made the right choice that day, then God would have had to take another route. Thank God, Abraham changed his thinking. We can change ours too, if we want to.

Erase the Doubt

It's up to each of us as individuals to refuse the cares of life. You can erase the tape recording of care in your mind with the tape eraser of the Word of God. You can erase the tapes of offense, negative thinking, wrong attitudes, complaining, and caring what people think about you. You can erase the wrong tapes by putting the Word of Almighty God in your heart, in your mind, and on your lips. When you do that, you will stand in the face of the devil and every care of life, saying, "I am victorious, I am well, I am healed, and I am prosperous! I will call things that are not as though they were. I will stand for God, I will live for God, and I will win in God!"

Praise God when the devil is knocking at the door and you can feel his hot breath on your neck. Praise God in the face of any circumstance. Praise Him when care tries to take hold of your mind. Praise Him in the morning, praise Him in the noonday, praise Him in the evening, and praise Him in the midnight hour. Praise Him as you lie on your bed. His praise should continually be in your mouth. Offer up a voice of thanksgiving and praise right now!

8

What You See Is What You Get

When the storms are howling, when the wind is blowing, when the dark clouds are over your head, what you see amid that storm is just as vital to your triumph as what you say.

Before the fiery trial ever arrived, Shadrach, Meshach, and Abednego saw their God as One Who would deliver them, *no matter what*. They saw their God unquestionably as a deliverer, but theirs was only one account of such faith.

In Daniel chapter 6, we see another man of faith in action. Daniel was a devout man of God who was devoted to prayer. This chapter in the Book of Daniel tells of Daniel's refusal to compromise his stand for God after his jealous peers tried to entrap him with an irreversible order from the king that banned prayer for 30 days.

DANIEL 6:7–10

7 All the presidents of the kingdom, the gov-
   ernors, and the princes, the counsellors
   and the captains, have consulted together
   to establish a royal statute, and to make a
   firm decree, that whosoever shall ask a
   petition of any God or man for thirty days,
   save of thee, O king, he shall be cast into
   the den of lions.

8 Now, O king, establish the decree, and sign
   the writing, that it be not changed, according to the law of the Medes and Persians,
   which altereth not."

9 Wherefore King Darius signed the writing
   and the decree.

10 Now when Daniel knew that the writing was
   signed, he went into his house; and his windows being opened in his chamber toward
   Jerusalem, he kneeled upon his knees three
   times a day, and prayed, and gave thanks
   before his God, as he did aforetime.

Notice what happened when Daniel heard that he
either had to worship the gods that this king had set up
or visit with the lions. Does the Bible say, "But when
Daniel knew that the writing was signed, he went into
his house and began to mourn"? Does it tell us "He
began to say, 'What have I done to deserve this? What in
the world is going on? How did I ever get myself in this
position? How in the world will I ever get out of this? Is
God even around? I don't feel like God is around' "?

No, the Bible doesn't say that. When he realized the decree had been signed, Daniel went into his house and prayed . . . with his windows *open.*

Let me stop here for a minute. Sometimes people come to me and say, "Brother Charles, troublesome things have come my way and they have so burdened me that I can't even pray." Well, if you have said that before, ask yourself this: What if someone who worshipped a false god told you, "If you don't worship my god, you will be thrown into a den of lions"? That would be a heavy burden too, wouldn't it? What would you do? You'd pray!

Daniel went into his house, kneeled three times a day, prayed, and gave thanks before his God, just as he had done *before* the new decree from the king. He didn't change one thing. He still kneeled and prayed three times a day!

Now I know the attitude of some people about prayer. You can almost hear some of them say to the Lord, "Now Lord, you know I took a promise card from the promise box this morning. Lord, you know after I gulped down that cup of coffee and the doughnut, I said a little prayer on the way out the door as I buttoned my coat. You do know I am busy. After all, I have to make a living."

But the Word says Daniel kneeled on his knees *three* times *every* day. To that, others might say, "Well now, you know, you want to be careful not to get too religious. Why, if you get *too* fanatical, it could affect your mind." One time a man said to me, "Brother Charles, I have heard of people going crazy reading the Bible." I said, "No, they were crazy before they started reading it."

What comment would you have made about that? The Bible didn't make them crazy; something was wrong with them before they started reading it. A *religious* thought (not a spiritual, Word-based one) is involved when people think they will be fanatical and out of balance if they get too serious about God. Some people think they need to be careful not to go too far, so if they think they are praying too much, they quit.

But Daniel, even in the middle of a challenging time, did not change from what he was already doing. Verse 10 says, "And he gave thanks before his God as he did aforetime."

Many times, fiery trials come and people try to jump in and do things they weren't doing before the fiery trial showed up. If you do that, the devil has the advantage. As I said earlier, by that time, the care is already in your house, lying on your couch with its shoes off . . . and it has your TV tuned to a program you don't like! Now you have to deal with it. And if you don't deal with it in the right way, it is going to defeat you. It doesn't matter how spiritual you are. It doesn't matter if you have 14 gifts from God. The care will defeat you if you do not know how to deal with it. Only when you take a steadfast stand of faith will God come on the scene for you as He did for Daniel. Let's read about how God showed up for him.

DANIEL 6:11–28

11 Then these men assembled, and found Daniel praying and making supplication before his God.

12 Then they came near, and spake before the king concerning the king's decree; Hast thou not signed a decree, that every man that shall ask a petition of any God or man within thirty days, save of thee, O king, shall be cast into the den of lions? The king answered and said, The thing is true, according to the law of the Medes and Persians, which altereth not.

13 Then answered they and said before the king, That Daniel, which is of the children of the captivity of Judah, regardeth not thee, O king, nor the decree that thou hast signed, but maketh his petition three times a day.

14 Then the king, when he heard these words, was sore displeased with himself, and set his heart on Daniel to deliver him: and he labored till the going down of the sun to deliver him.

15 Then these men assembled unto the king, and said unto the king, Know, O king, that the law of the Medes and Persians is, That no decree nor statute which the king establisheth may be changed.

16 Then the king commanded, and they brought Daniel, and cast him into the den of lions. Now the king spake and said unto Daniel, Thy God whom thou servest continually, he will deliver thee.

17 And a stone was brought, and laid upon the mouth of the den; and the king sealed it with his own signet, and with the signet of his lords; that the purpose might not be changed concerning Daniel.

18 Then the king went to his palace, and passed the night fasting: neither were instruments of music brought before him: and his sleep went from him.

19 Then the king arose very early in the morning, and went in haste unto the den of lions.

20 And when he came to the den, he cried with a lamentable voice unto Daniel: and the king spake and said to Daniel, O Daniel, servant of the living God, is thy God, whom thou servest continually, able to deliver thee from the lions?

21 Then said Daniel unto the king, O king, live forever.

22 My God hath sent his angel, and hath shut the lions' mouths, that they have not hurt me: forasmuch as before him innocency was found in me; and also before thee, O king, have I done no hurt.

23 Then was the king exceeding glad for him, and commanded that they should take

Daniel up out of the den. So Daniel was taken up out of the den, and no manner of hurt was found upon him, because he believed in his God.

24 And the king commanded, and they brought those men which had accused Daniel, and they cast them into the den of lions, them, their children, and their wives; and the lions had the mastery of them, and brake all their bones in pieces or ever they came at the bottom of the den.

25 Then king Darius wrote unto all people, nations, and languages, that dwell in all the earth; Peace be multiplied unto you.

26 I make a decree, That in every dominion of my kingdom men tremble and fear before the God of Daniel: for he is the living God, and steadfast forever, and his kingdom that which shall not be destroyed, and his dominion shall be even unto the end.

27 He delivereth and rescueth, and he worketh signs and wonders in heaven and in earth, who hath delivered Daniel from the power of the lions.

28 So this Daniel prospered in the reign of Darius, and in the reign of Cyrus the Persian.

Daniel was not hurt in any manner "because he believed in his God" (v. 23)! But look at what happened to his accusers and their families (who, by the way, didn't believe in his God). Verse 24 says, ". . . *and they cast them into the den of lions, them, their children, and*

*their wives; and the lions had the mastery of them, and
broke all their bones in pieces or ever they came at the
bottom of the den."*

Now let's look at Daniel's attitude toward the king
during this trial. Verse 21 says Daniel spoke from the
lions' den, saying, ". . . *O king, live forever."*

If we had been in that den of lions, we might have
thought, *You rascal king, you, I'm going to pull you
down here with me and let these lions sniff you a while.*
But Daniel didn't think that. He simply responded
with "O king, live forever." How could he respond that
way? Because he knew going into that den of lions,
what God would do. Just like the three Hebrew children,
Daniel saw his God only as a deliverer—he never
changed what he saw, from the beginning of the trial
to the end.

Seeing Is Believing

The word *see* means "to construct a mental image."
Now some people may think, *Wait a minute, Brother
Charles, you are getting into the mind-control area.*
They think of mental images as belonging to the reli-
gions of the mind, trying to approach God from a men-
tal standpoint. But that is not it at all.

You must be born again in your spirit to become a
child and a temple of God. Once you do that, then you
have to do something with your mind. Your mind is not
and cannot be born again, but it can be renewed. It is

up to you to train your mind to align with the Word of God. If you don't do the right thing with your mind, your life as a child of God will be miserable.

Your mind must be renewed to think and believe the Word of God if you want to overcome the problems in your home, on your job, with people, or with life in general.

Paint Pictures

The word *see* also means "to accept or imagine as acceptable." We know that all words paint pictures. When you buy a book to read, every word in that book is designed to paint a picture of what the author wishes to portray to you.

Meditating on the Word of God paints a picture for us in our thinking so that the spirit of our mind is renewed through that picture. We alone decide whether we will meditate on the Word enough to develop a picture in our mind. And we alone decide whether to accept or reject that picture. If we accept and hold fast to the Word picture, we will win; if we reject the picture, we will lose.

Meditate Your Way to Victory

The first thing you must learn when the fiery trial comes is, don't be alarmed or frightened. If fear is your first reaction, you have immediately removed yourself from faith. Faith and fear are like oil and water; they can't operate together in the same vessel at the same time. Fear paints the wrong picture and leads to an undesirable outcome. Neither the Hebrew boys nor Daniel responded in fear, though their circumstances looked grim. When circumstances look impossible, an image of victory will dispel fear and make a way for faith to develop.

God sees you as victorious in *all* things. And the more you meditate and read God's Word and fellowship with Him in prayer, the more you will begin to develop images of victory in your trials. But meditating on God's Word must be a lifestyle in order for you to maintain an image of yourself as a winner.

Joshua 1:8 says, *"This book of the law shall not depart out of thy mouth; but thou shalt meditate therein day and night, that thou mayest observe to do according to all that is written therein: for then thou shalt make thy way prosperous, and then thou shalt have good success."* Now can you understand why God told Joshua that he should meditate in His Word day and night? God wants His people to be prosperous and have good success.

And this verse tells us something else important. God also said to meditate in His Word day and night so that we may "observe to do all that is written therein." So meditating on the Word helps us *do* the Word.

The Bible says if we make a lifestyle of meditating on the Word, then our way will be prosperous, we will have good success, and we will do all that is written therein. Now that sounds like winning in life, doesn't it?

The Book of Joshua tells us to meditate in God's Word day and night so that an image can be painted on the inside of us of how great God is. We can have that picture so clearly defined inside of us that it is all we can see.

No matter what comes your way, you can have this picture on the inside of you of how great your God is, and it can run on the large screen in the cinema of your life. The picture can be so large and clear and strong on the inside of you that fiery trials can't even get in the theater door, much less go to the popcorn stand or find a seat!

We have to get up off our pity-party seat and begin to let God's Word develop images of victory in our lives. If we don't, we will drown in our tears!

Follow Peace

It is very important for you, as a child of God, to see yourself as a winner when defeat lies in wait. You need to see yourself teamed up with God, and you need to see yourself as an overcomer.

John 16:33 says, *"These things I have spoken unto you, that in me ye might have peace. In the world ye shall have tribulation: but be of good cheer; I have overcome the world."* Here Jesus says that despite our tribulation, we can have peace.

Sometimes people only read the part of this verse that says, "In the world you shall have tribulation." They think, *Yes, dear Lord, that is true.* Why, I have even seen people cry and shout over that. They would say, "Yes, you know the Bible says in the world you will have tribulation," and then they would shout about it! But that wasn't all Jesus said. Before He spoke of tribulation, He assured us that, in Him, we could have peace.

Let's look at John 16:33 again to see something else: *"These things I have spoken unto you, that in me ye might have peace. In the world ye shall have tribulation: BUT BE OF GOOD CHEER; I have overcome the world."*

Jesus told us to be of good cheer. You can't be of good cheer unless you have the right picture in your mind. Going into a fiery trial, you must see your victory. If you had been in Daniel's shoes and all you could see was that lion licking his lips, you would just have been a good meal for him. He would have asked the blessing before he got to you!

What you see is determined by your faith in the oracles of God. If your faith is in God, His sayings will determine what you see. *"If any man speak, let him speak as the oracles of God . . ."* (1 Peter 4:11). What did the Hebrew children do? They spoke according to the Word of their God. What did Daniel do? He spoke according to the Word of his God. Why? Because they had learned to trust God. They knew He would back what He said. They knew His integrity was without flaw.

In Christ

Jesus tells us to be of good cheer in the middle of tribulation in the world because He overcame the world! Now some have thought, *Well, that's fine for You, Jesus; but, what about me? Where are You tonight when I need You?*

Let me tell you where He is.

Galatians 2:20 says, *"I am crucified with Christ: nevertheless I live; yet not I, but Christ liveth in me: and the life which I now live in the flesh I live by the faith of the Son of God, who loved me, and gave himself for me."*

Say this to yourself: *I am in Christ and Christ is in me. If Christ has overcome the world, then I am in the middle of the Overcomer. If Christ is in me, the Overcomer is on the inside of me. I can speak as the oracles of God and say with certainty: Greater is He that is in me than he that is in the world.*

You and I can say that because He is in us, and we are in Him. We can say that because it is the oracle of *God*; it is a saying of God. He had it recorded in the Bible to help us know that Jesus is bigger than any of our trials.

When Daniel went to his house, opened his window, looked toward Jerusalem, and prayed to his God, he saw his God as *bigger* than his tribulation. The lions were not even a consideration to him. The fiery furnace was heated seven times hotter than normal for the three Hebrew boys, and even the men who threw them in perished; yet the furnace was no consideration to them. The Hebrew children had a party in the *middle* of the fiery furnace, and Jesus showed up for the party!

Daniel 3:24–25 says, *"Then Nebuchadnezzar the king was astonied, and rose up in haste, and spake, and said unto his counsellors, Did not we cast three men bound into the midst of the fire? They answered and said unto the king, True, O king. He answered and said, Lo, I see four men loose, walking in the midst of the fire, and they have no hurt; and the form of the fourth is like the Son of God."*

Jesus said that in the world you will have tribulation—which can be anything that troubles, distresses, worries, disturbs, agitates, or urges you to take the care of it—but He also said He has overcome it all, and He is in you!

Letting Go

What do you see concerning the cares you are dealing with today? Do you see God as *bigger* than your problems? If not, you need to make adjustments immediately.

In life, you *have* to let go of certain things. You must let go of the memory of things people do to you. You must let go of the memory of some things people say about you. They might call you names and demean you and even slander you, but you still must let these things go. Many people have gone through divorce, and maybe you are one of them. If so, you must let it go and move on with your life. Get it behind you. If you don't let it go, it will become a care.

Situations like these may have brought care into your life, and perhaps you find yourself in a certain set of circumstances today because of them. If that is what you are dealing with, then ask yourself what image

you have in your mind. Ask yourself what tape is playing there. And if those images and the recordings on
that tape don't agree with the Word of God, then begin
to use the Word of God to change what you see and hear.

Loosen the Bands

S ometimes we have to deal with the cares of life because of unexpected and unjust assaults. The Bible gives us a story of triumph in that kind of adversity and unexpected hardship. In Paul and Silas' ordeal in the Philippian jail, we can see how important our actions are when we find ourselves in the midst of an unexpected trial.

Though they did nothing but preach and set a young girl free from a spirit of divination, Paul and Silas ended up beaten and thrown into the worst part of the prison. Let's look at their story:

ACTS 16:16–26

16 And it came to pass, as we went to prayer, a certain damsel possessed with a spirit of divination met us, which brought her masters much gain by soothsaying:

17 The same followed Paul and us, and cried, saying, These men are the servants of the most high God, which shew unto us the way of salvation.

18 And this did she many days. But Paul, being grieved, turned and said to the spirit, I command thee in the name of Jesus Christ to come out of her. And he came out the same hour.

19 And when her masters saw that the hope of their gains was gone, they caught Paul and Silas, and drew them into the marketplace unto the rulers,

20 And brought them to the magistrates, saying, These men, being Jews, do exceedingly trouble our city,

21 And teach customs, which are not lawful for us to receive, neither to observe, being Romans.

22 And the multitude rose up together against them: and the magistrates rent off their clothes, and commanded to beat them.

23 And when they had laid many stripes upon them, they cast them into prison, charging the jailor to keep them safely:

24 Who, having received such a charge, thrust them into the inner prison, and made their feet fast in the stocks.

25 And at midnight Paul and Silas prayed, and sang praises unto God: and the prisoners heard them.

26 And suddenly there was a great earthquake, so that the foundations of the prison were shaken: and immediately all the doors were opened, and every one's bands were loosed.

An opportunity for taking upon themselves the cares of life had presented itself to Paul and Silas. They were beaten, their backs were bleeding, and their feet were in stocks.

Sometimes people say, "You know, Brother Charles, my situation is so heavy on me I just don't know what to do." Well, Paul and Silas found themselves in a heavy situation too, but at that midnight hour, they knew what to do. They prayed. And then they sang praises unto God!

Now look at how God responded to their praying and singing. Verse 26 says that suddenly a great earthquake shook the foundations of the prison, *". . . and immediately all the doors were opened, and every one's bands were loosed."*

Jailhouse Rock

God just suddenly showed up! All of a sudden, the jailhouse began rocking. It was a Holy Ghost jailhouse rock!

As the jail rocked, the stocks on their feet began shaking, the doors opened, and Paul and Silas were free. When the jailer was about to take his own life because he thought his prisoners had escaped, Paul stopped him.

ACTS 16:27–34

27 And the keeper of the prison awaking out of his sleep, and seeing the prison doors open, he drew out his sword, and would have killed himself, supposing that the prisoners had been fled.

28 But Paul cried with a loud voice, saying, Do thyself no harm: for we are all here.

29 Then he called for a light, and sprang in, and came trembling, and fell down before Paul and Silas,

30 And brought them out, and said, Sirs, what must I do to be saved?

31 And they said, Believe on the Lord Jesus Christ, and thou shalt be saved, and thy house.

32 And they spake unto him the word of the Lord, and to all that were in his house.

33 And he took them the same hour of the night, and washed their stripes; and was baptized, he and all his, straightway.

34 And when he had brought them into his house, he set meat before them, and rejoiced, believing in God with all his house.

Paul and Silas turned that bad situation into a prayer and praise meeting! They turned around the cares of life and they beat the devil.

And that's not all! Their strong stand for God inspired others to want to serve God.

Just as Paul and Silas did, you can defeat the devil when the cares of life come unexpectedly. Say this to yourself: "I can defeat the devil! I not only *can* defeat the devil, I *do* defeat the devil. I refuse to be full of care. I refuse to be worried, anxious, or moved out of God's place for me. Jesus will not find me with care when He comes."

11

Unaware

As we have seen, mere formulas of faith will not withstand the onslaught of trouble when it comes. Only a lifestyle of faith will see us through.

Satan comes with all of the cares of this life for the purpose of occupying our mind and distracting us so that we will be out of our place and the Day of the Lord will come on us unawares. He wants us in a place God has not designed or willed for us. (Many preachers are there.) When we are out of place, we will have no peace; we will be overcharged with care.

When you are preoccupied with cares, you become unaware of how quickly the events in God's timetable are passing. You are focused on the cares that have set up residence in your heart or mind, and you become dull to the voice of the Holy Spirit and dull to the sound and

Word of God. You are out there in a place where you can't hear God speaking into your life. And that is exactly where the devil wants you.)

Many people, when they are overcharged with care, stop going to church. I see people in this generation and time who once were faithful in church, but they are not faithful now. Something has distracted them and, little by little, they have become too busy. They are shaking and moving; they are doing *stuff.* Care is encumbering and distracting their lives as it moves in and occupies their mind, overcharging them with situations. Faithfulness to God is not important to them anymore. Why? They have become encumbered by the cares of this life. They may be saying, "Hallelujah, Glory to God, I love You, Jesus," but they are dull of hearing and out of place. God can't work and move through them as He wants to because they have disconnected His power, joy, and peace from their life.

Before the End . . .

All of God's people are to be involved in a last-day revival, not just the apostles, prophets, evangelists, pastors, and teachers. The Holy Ghost is going to be poured out in a *double measure.* The former and latter outpouring of the Holy Ghost is coming to this earth in a way that has never been seen—more than was seen on the Day of Pentecost and more than in the years since the Day of Pentecost.

We need to be in our God-called positions _right now_, for it is clear in the following passage of Scripture that we are nearing the end of God's timetable:

LUKE 21:5–9

5   And as some spake of the temple, how it was adorned with goodly stones and gifts, he said,

6   As for these things which ye behold, the days will come, in the which there shall not be left one stone upon another, that shall not be thrown down.

7   And they asked him, saying, Master, but when shall these things be? and what sign will there be when these things shall come to pass?

8   And he said, Take heed that ye be not deceived: for many shall come in my name, saying, I am Christ; and the time draweth near: go ye not therefore after them.

9   But when ye shall hear of wars and commotions, be not terrified: for these things must first come to pass; but the end is not by and by.

Jesus addresses quite a time span here. First, he speaks of the destruction of the temple (v. 6), which would happen in that day. Then He moves across the span of time to _our_ day, the time in which we are living now. He said there would be wars and commotions. And He told us when we hear of these, we should not be terrified, for these things must come to pass . . . before the end.

Kingdom Against Kingdom

Luke 21:10 says, *"Then said he unto them, Nation shall rise against nation, and kingdom against kingdom."* Here Jesus is speaking both of the time frame in which we live and of the years preceding our time. As it is used here, the Greek word translated *nation* is the same word from which we get our word *ethnic*. So Jesus was talking about race rising against race.

We know that in the world today animosity, prejudice, and discrimination exist among people. We hear about the problems between races of people and the prejudice among nations of the world.

Jesus said all of this would be a sign of the last days when the devil would be stirring up people to divert their attention from God and keep them at odds with one another. Jesus prophesied this over two thousand years ago. He said nation shall rise against nation, and kingdom against kingdom. He said great earthquakes, famines, and pestilences shall appear in many places. We see all of that today; these things are happening all around us. Sadly, they are happening with such frequency that we don't pay as much attention to them as we once did. They have become commonplace.

Read on and see if this is a picture of our world today:

LUKE 21:11–17

11 And great earthquakes shall be in divers places, and famines, and pestilences; and

fearful sights and great signs shall there be
from heaven.

12 But before all these, they shall lay their
hands on you, and persecute you, delivering you up to the synagogues, and into pris-
ons, being brought before kings and rulers
for my name's sake.

13 And it shall turn to you for a testimony.

14 Settle it therefore in your hearts, not to
meditate before what ye shall answer:

15 For I will give you a mouth and wisdom,
which all your adversaries shall not be able
to gainsay nor resist.

16 And ye shall be betrayed both by parents,
and brethren, and kinsfolk, and friends;
and some of you shall they cause to be put
to death.

17 And ye shall be hated of all men for my
name's sake.

Christians are hated all around the world.

And even in the United States, many are trying to
take Jesus out of our schools, courthouses, and other
public places. The same move is coming against the rest
of God's Word, such as the Ten Commandments. Some
people do not have enough sense to know that if everyone would just adhere to the Ten Commandments, we
would live in a great society. Man's plan for a great society has never worked without the input of God's Word.

Despite the animosity toward Christians, we are
destined to win—if our faith is in God. Although all the

prophecies *must* be fulfilled, God's faithful people will be protected through obedience and faith in Him. Jesus tells us not to be afraid—He will see us through.

The Times of the Gentiles Fulfilled

In 1948, we saw Israel reestablished and recognized as a nation, signifying that in God's timetable, the times of the Gentiles were nearing fulfillment. Luke 21:24 says, *". . . and Jerusalem shall be trodden down of the Gentiles, until the times of the Gentiles be fulfilled."* In 1967, we saw Israel move into Jerusalem.

I believe we can trace the beginning of the times of the Gentiles back to the tenth chapter of Acts. As recorded in that chapter, Peter had a vision and fell into a trance on a rooftop one day, and God showed him how he would go beyond the boundaries of the nation of Israel and reach out to all people all over the world. When Israel, God's chosen people, rejected Jesus of Nazareth and refused to receive Him as their Messiah, the proclamation of the Gospel then focused primarily on the Gentile world.

The Book of Acts says Cornelius was one of those Gentiles. He was a devout and just man, and he was in fasting and prayer before the Lord when God told him to send some of his servants to Joppa to get Peter.

Peter, having heard from God to go preach the Gospel to the Gentiles, went with Cornelius' servants,

arrived at Cornelius' house, and began to preach. And
the Bible says that as those gathered there heard the
words that Peter preached, the Holy Ghost fell on
them. They received the Holy Ghost and were born
again. This opened the door of salvation to the Gentiles
(_see_ Acts 15:1–31). But now with the return of Israel to
their ancestral homeland, I believe we can see the clos-
ing of the Gentile age on the horizon (Acts 10; 15:14).
(To avoid confusion, let me say that this is a reference to
God's timetable only—_anyone_ can still be saved.)

The hour of the Second Coming is imminent. Jesus
said in Luke 21:25–27, _"And there shall be signs in the
sun, and in the moon, and in the stars; and upon the
earth distress of nations, with perplexity; the sea and
the waves roaring; Men's hearts failing them for fear,
and for looking after those things which are coming on
the earth: for the powers of heaven shall be shaken. And
then shall they see the Son of man coming in a cloud
with power and great glory."_

When Jesus ascended into Heaven after He was
raised from the dead, two angels appeared to those
who watched Him go up. The angels said, _". . . Ye men
of Galilee, why stand ye gazing up into heaven? this
same Jesus, which is taken up from you into heaven,
shall so come in like manner as ye have seen him go
into heaven"_ (Acts 1:11).

This verse says Jesus was taken away on a cloud,
and Luke 21:27 says He will come back in the same

manner. He is coming back on a cloud. In Luke 21:28 Jesus stated, *"And when these things begin to come to pass, then look up, and lift up your heads; for your redemption draweth nigh."*

This verse doesn't say, "When these things come to pass, be discouraged and full of care." No, it says to look up, for our redemption draweth nigh. What did Jesus mean by "draweth nigh"? He meant when you see all of these other things happening, you will know that the Second Coming is about to happen. So look up, and expect to see Him.

Luke's account of the Gospel goes on to tell us more about the signs of the Second Coming in our generation:

LUKE 21:29–32

29 **And he spake to them a parable: Behold the fig tree, and all the trees;**

30 **When they now shoot forth, ye see and know of your own selves that summer is now nigh at hand.**

31 **So likewise ye, when ye see these things come to pass, know ye that the kingdom of God is nigh at hand.**

32 **Verily I say unto you, This generation shall not pass away, till all be fulfilled.**

Now notice that when Jesus says "this generation," He is talking to the generation that sees these things. Which generation will see these things? I believe it is ours. We will see them. He is saying that we will see these things happen, and when we do, we should know that the coming of the Lord is nigh at hand.

I believe this generation is going to see the return of the Lord! Now I'm not saying _everyone_ around us today is going to see the face-to-face return of the Lord, but I am saying that some in this generation will be alive and see His return.

Some who are alive today will see the Lord descend from Heaven with a shout and with the voice of the archangel and the trump of God. Some who are alive today will see the dead in Christ raised and living believers changed in a moment, in the twinkling of an eye. Then we will all be caught up together in the clouds to meet the Lord (_see_ 1 Cor. 15:52; 1 Thess. 4:16,17). What a glorious day!

The Day of the Lord

Jesus warned us that we would be tempted to take on the cares of life as we see the day approaching. In Luke 21:33 and 34, He says, *"Heaven and earth shall pass away: but my words shall not pass away. And take heed to yourselves, lest at any time your hearts be overcharged with surfeiting, and drunkenness, and cares of this life, and so that day come upon you unawares."*

When Jesus said "so that day come upon you unawares," He was not saying that if it catches you unaware, you won't go to Heaven, because if you're saved, you are born again and the Holy Spirit lives on the inside of you. You are a child of God and you will go to Heaven. He was saying that if you are being distracted with the cares of life, you will be out of position. You will not be in your place, at your post, where God needs and wants you to be. Cares will have occupied and seized your mind.

Care will be pulling your mind in different directions through worry and anxiety about different matters of life.

You will be out of position because if you are over-charged with cares, your mind will be drawn and dis-tracted and you will, come to the place where you can't hear from God. Your mind can be so clouded with worry and care that you can't hear His voice. When you are in that place, you will make decisions based not on the Spirit of God but on what looks best for you in the natural. You will miss God.

Satan also knows we will not be in position for God to use us in that exciting time if we are overcharged with cares. That's what the flood of cares in our day is all about. Satan has already suffered a humiliating defeat at the hands of Jesus. He doesn't want to think about the day Jesus will show up again in power and great glory, and he doesn't want us to think about it either. He knows he is headed for the lake of fire, but he hasn't surrendered to that yet. Today he wants to wreak as much havoc in our life as he can.

But the good news is, we can refuse to allow Satan to do that. We can refuse to allow our mind to be trou-bled. We can turn our heart toward the Lord's return and listen for God to direct us. We can make a decision right now to maximize every moment before we hear that great voice from Heaven say, "Come up hither!"

Light Your Fire

If there was ever a day when our spiritual fire should be lit, it is today. If there was ever a day when we should be sincere and fervent about the things of God, it is this day in which we live. If there was ever a day when we need to make ourselves available to the Holy Ghost and to Jesus, the Head of the Church, to do whatever He wills to do in us, it is this day, hour, time, and moment. We can't afford to be downcast now. This is the greatest moment the Body of Christ will know on the earth.

Jesus is coming for a people who are different from the world. He is coming for a people who are not bowed down with the cares of the world. He is coming for a people who have lifted up their heads and who know their redemption is drawing nigh.

We must not think or be like the rest of the world. We are in the world, but we are not of the world. We are to be different from people who are lost and without Jesus Christ. We are different because we are saved; we are redeemed.

Romans 12:2 says, *"And be not conformed to this world: but be ye transformed by the renewing of your mind, that ye may prove what is that good, and acceptable, and perfect, will of God."* In this verse, Paul says we can prove the good, acceptable, and perfect will of God. That means we are to think as we are supposed to think so God can work His will in us and His plan through us.

Our faith, like that of Daniel and the three Hebrews boys, should cause people without Jesus Christ to take notice and turn to our God. If we are wringing our hands right along with those who don't know God or don't serve Him, why would they be interested in knowing our God? They wouldn't.

Jesus does not want any of His people burdened with care. He commands us in His Word to cast our care upon Him, because He cares for us (1 Peter 5:7). We are instructed to be careful for nothing, but in everything, by prayer and supplication with thanksgiving, to let our requests be made known to God (Phil. 4:6) He has provided everything we need to be examples of His goodness and mercy, and to disentangle ourselves from the pressures of life. We are living in an exciting time!

Conclusion

If you are born again, the Holy Spirit lives on the inside of you, and you are qualified for Heaven. But that doesn't mean that you will automatically live in victory in this life, nor does it make you interested in the things of God. Though the Bible record of the Second Coming is important, you don't lift up your head just because you read scriptures that say Jesus is coming back. But adhering to spiritual principles will cause you to lift up your head and walk right into a place of victory, available for God to prove His good, acceptable, and perfect will for you. That will happen as you set your affection on that which is above, not on which is on the earth.

In this book, we have seen how to overcome the cares of life. If you hold fast to these spiritual principles, you will successfully deal with them. Make up your mind today that you will be on the lookout for cares of life that are trying to come in and dominate your thinking. If you find yourself downcast, pick yourself up and, instead of worrying, make it your lifestyle to do these things:

☞ Meditate in God's Word day and night.

☞ Let the Word construct images of victory in your mind.

☞ Cast down any imagination that contradicts the Word.

☞ Refuse the cares of life.

☞ Speak the Word instead of the circumstances.

☞ Trust God.

God has things He wants you to accomplish, but you can't accomplish them if you are laden with care. If the day of the Lord's return catches you unawares and out of position, you won't be ready and available to Him. But if you will be diligent to practice what is set forth in this book, you will rise above the cares of life. You will not be burdened by the heaviness of life, and you will be in a place where God can call upon you at any moment for the purpose of His Kingdom.

When we focus on God's spiritual principles, we will live out these last days being useful to Him. When we see to it that our heart is not troubled or afraid, our very lifestyle will cause men to consider living for the one—and only—true and living God.

Though it's easy to follow the world into despair, you are different from the world. Lift up your head! Your redemption is nearer than you think!

About the Author

After graduating from RHEMA Bible Training Center in 1975, Charles Cowan moved to Nashville, Tennessee, where he pioneered Faith Is The Victory Church. Rev. Cowan continues to pastor the church, which has grown to 2,000 members and reaches out to minister to the whole family.

Rev. Cowan teaches the Word of God with a practical simplicity that is useful for daily living. Through his teaching, he helps the believer learn how to live a victorious life of faith in God.

During his ministry of over thirty-five years, Rev. Cowan has taught in churches throughout the United States and helped train national pastors in India, the Philippines, Sweden, Norway, Finland, Grenada, Honduras, Estonia, and Canada. He has also taught in ministers' training schools in the Czech Republic, Italy, and England.

To contact the author, write:
Charles Cowan
Faith Is The Victory Church
3344 Walton Lane
P.O. Box 160268
Nashville, TN 37216
www.victoriousliving.org